The Mechanical Patient

The Mechanical Patient

Finding a More Human
Model of Health

Sholom Glouberman

Routledge
Taylor & Francis Group

A PRODUCTIVITY PRESS BOOK

Routledge
Taylor & Francis Group
711 Third Avenue, New York, NY 10017

© 2018 by Taylor & Francis Group, LLC
Productivity Press is an imprint of Taylor & Francis Group, an Informa business

No claim to original U.S. Government works

Printed on acid-free paper

International Standard Book Number-13: 978-1-138-54994-4 (Hardback)
International Standard Book Number-13: 978-0-429-49033-0 (eBook)

Library of Congress Cataloging-in-Publication Data

Names: Glouberman, S., author.
Title: The mechanical patient : finding a more human model of health / Sholom Glouberman.
Description: Boca Raton : Taylor & Francis, 2018. | Includes bibliographical references and index. |
Identifiers: LCCN 2018002700 (print) | LCCN 2018017943 (ebook) | ISBN 9780429490330 (eBook) | ISBN 9781138549944 (hardback : alk. paper)
Subjects: LCSH: Medicine--Philosophy. | Health--History.
Classification: LCC R723 (ebook) | LCC R723 .G57 2018 (print) | DDC 610.1--dc23
LC record available at https://lccn.loc.gov/2018002700

Visit the Taylor & Francis Web site at
http://www.taylorandfrancis.com

and the Productivity Press site at
http://www.ProductivityPress.com

This book is dedicated with love to
Susan, Misha, Margaux, and Billy

Contents

List of Figures

List of Tables

Acknowledgments

This book connects philosophical and historical ideas with healthcare issues. I believe that this somewhat conceptual look at problems in healthcare leads to new and valuable insights. I had for some time recognized that the philosophical underpinnings of the medical model enabled doctors and others to separate us from our bodies. But I had not yet realized that the mechanical patient is a product of seventeenth century philosophy—that the very idea of the modern patient was tied to the concept of people as chemical/mechanical bodies. Luckily, I received a grant from the Change Foundation in Toronto to pursue this topic. I used it to collect and review the material essential to this book.

My interest in how patients are treated led me to found a patients' organization called Patients Canada, Toronto, Ontario. We tried with some success to bring the patient perspective to healthcare. While seriously ill I was excluded from the organization. And so, I came back to the material I had collected and began to unravel the sources of our current ideas about patients. This became an exciting return to my philosophical beginnings. My brother-in-law, Chaim Tannenbaum, gave me a book by Paul Horwich, *Wittgenstein's Metaphilosophy*, that helped me see how much traditional mistaken views in philosophy affected the current medical practice.

Many of my friends and colleagues helped. They worked through early drafts and helped me articulate the notion of the mechanical patient. There are many people to thank.

Ruth Portner read every draft to improve the clarity and shape of the text. Orlando Buonastella, Harry Burns, Murray Enkin, Gail Kaufman, Gary Kraemer, Elizabeth Mulley Terry Picton, Andrea Shewchuck, and James Wilk read versions and their honest comments and unfettered criticisms were instrumental in making a better book. David Stover published a second edition of my early book *Keepers* and he, Daniel Baird, Sheila Heti, James Fitzgerald, and Pat Crean gave me excellent and detailed advice about publishing this book. Cedric Cruz checked the references, helped me prepare the bibliography, and kept my library of books and papers usable through somewhat chaotic flurries of work.

Some of my friends, David Berlin, Debbie Kirshner, Peter Mulley, Sheila Damon, Peter Moss, Phyllis Platt, Brian Clark, David Streiner, Steve Herbert, Marsha Herbert, Evan Blue, Alma Petchersky, Alex Tarnopolsky, Margaret Anne Fitzpatrick, Charles Hanly Alan Engelstad, Alison Fleming, Joan Moss, Earl Berger, Gerrry Portner, Laura Alper, Laszlo Barna, Carol Kitai, Dan Perlitz, Mary Collier, Jo Boufford, Normand Rinfret, Phyllis Yaffe, Francie Kendall, Louise Lemieux Charles, Berl Schiff, Gissa Gold Schiff, Keith Oatley, and Jennifer Jenkins, listened to my ramblings about the book which were at first almost unintelligible. They helped me calm down, take my time, and encouraged me to continue.

It was easy and straightforward working with Kristine Mednansky and Angela Graven from Routledge who made the physical book possible.

I gave a number of talks based on the book that helped me see what needed to be better articulated. Thanks to the Registered Nurses' Association of Ontario, the Canadian Association of Enterstomal Therapy, The Ontario Nursing Informatics Group, Michael Carter of the University of Toronto Faculty of Bio-Engineering, and Leslie Breitner, director of the International Masters for Health Leadership at McGill University. We held a small conference at Baycrest Health Sciences led by Jennifer LaTrobe and Tim Casswell using discussion and visual minutes to consider the pathways to change. About 15 people came and showed us how necessary it was to limit the scope of the investigation.

Damian Tarnopolsky supplied useful advice and published a chapter of an early version of the book in the *Toronto Review of Books*. The late Brenda Zimmerman and I wrote a report for the Romanow Commission on complexity in healthcare some years ago and her ideas have certainly helped me to clarify my understanding of the place of patients in chronic disease management.

My wife and true love, Susan Glouberman, was with me all the way: She read every word many times and encouraged me when it did not go well. Nochem and Dina Glouberman, Chaim Tannenbaum and Susannah Phillips, and Mark Glouberman provided familial support. My son Misha kept telling me to make the book shorter and more readable. He, Margaux Williamson, and our grandson Billy gave us the love and close family that make for a good and happy life.

Author

Sholom Glouberman is a philosopher in Residence at Baycrest Health Sciences in Toronto, Canada. He has a PhD in philosophy from Cornell, Ithaca, New York. His early experience in healthcare was caring for his dying father. Since then, he's been a planner and adviser at teaching hospitals, has headed think tanks, and lectured at universities in Canada, the UK, and the US. He's been a fellow at the King's Fund in London, the New York Academy of Medicine, and is a founder of Patients Canada, Toronto, Canada. He has written five books, many articles, and spoken before audiences around the world. In 2015, Sholom underwent a major surgical procedure and became a patient. His direct experience and work with others has helped him to see the disparity between the medical model and patient concerns.

Chapter 1

Introduction

The medical model that informs the training of doctors and the care of patients considers people to be machines with organs, limbs, and chemical processes. Wikipedia, for example, says that health is "the level of functional and metabolic efficiency of a living organism." In plain language, health is the extent to which our limbs and organs work well, and the degree to which we are able to properly digest our food. Medical examinations are surveys of the chemical and mechanical systems of our bodies. We are mechanical patients.

There have been only two Western medical models since antiquity: Galen's humoral model and the current mechanical model, which was initiated in the seventeenth century. This model became the primary standard for medical education and practice only in the late nineteenth century. Today the mechanical model is so well established that medical interventions repair the damaged mechanical body through ever more technically complex surgery, and pharmacological innovations maintain and heal the diseased chemical processes of the mechanical patient.

It was only in the late twentieth century that the model of the mechanical patient began to display serious deficiencies. As western populations aged and more diseases were identified as chronic rather than infectious, it emerged that social and relational factors are critical to health along with the chemical and mechanical ones. However, the model for health-care education and treatment has not kept pace and remains resistant to change. The concept of the mechanical patient has been so deeply embedded in our thinking that when patients and practitioners have strong feelings that something is wrong, they have some difficulty expressing their reservations. Simply arguing against the current situation has done little good.

The model has been so successful that it has at times even confused health with happiness. According to these versions of the model, if we eat well, exercise sufficiently, and are properly vaccinated, then, barring any genetically caused diseases, we should be healthy *and* happy. At any indication of unhappiness, we are offered treatment: either a chemical drug to directly change our mood or a surgical procedure to respond to the organ or limb that we are unhappy about.

The Mechanical Patient disentangles the issues associated with the model. It clarifies how we got to this point and suggests responses to the exaggerated place of the mechanical model in our society. It presents a historical and conceptual background that describes how the chemical/mechanical model took the place of the earlier Galenic humoral account and gained control of our thinking about health. The book develops strong arguments for a more humanized way of understanding health and its place in our lives, outlines some of its features, and joins a growing movement to go beyond our current chemical/mechanical orientation.

There is a need for a book with this perspective. Atul Gawande's *Being Mortal* describes the inhumane treatment of old people in nursing homes. Gawande explains that these homes were created on the model of hospitals and as a result do not provide a homelike comforting environment. He urges widespread reform. But there is little explanation of why the chemical/mechanical treatment of patients in *hospitals* was adopted in the first place and, indeed, whether it is entirely appropriate. *The Mechanical Patient* provides this necessary conceptual context. It demonstrates how once the machine became the dominant medical model, there was little choice but to provide hospital patients (and also nursing home residents) with the safest and most up-to-date chemical/mechanical environment. It was thought that support for their social/relational needs would automatically follow once they regain their health in a properly designed institution. Understanding their origin is important if we are to create more humane hospitals and nursing homes. Revising the mechanical medical model is a necessary contributor to such changes. Better appreciation of the limited contribution of chemical/mechanical health to overall health, and that mechanical health is just one of many contributors to a good life, is the critical aim of this book.

The *Mechanical Patient* begins with an account of the origins of the first Western medical model. Galen's humoral medicine owed much to Aristotelian science and ethics. Aristotle recognized that health is one of many social/relational resources for a good life. The humoral model, as developed by Galen, used the medical writings of Hippocrates and the philosophical and scientific views of Aristotle to declare that good health is highly individualized and depends upon an appropriate balance of four humors specific to each patient. Humoral remedies remain in use today: We still go to spas that had their origins in antiquity, and drink *hot* soups for *colds*. This recollection of an earlier model lets us see how much we internalize ideas without really knowing where they come from or if they are even true. We are surprised when it emerges that the Galenic model of the patient was intrinsic to most medical education and practice until quite recently— medical patients were routinely cupped, purged, and bled by doctors until the twentieth century.

Modern medicine functions in direct contradiction to Galen's theory. It is derived from a seventeenth century philosophical idea of the standard mechanical patient.

The Mechanical Patient tells us how the chemical aspect of the model evolved from Renaissance alchemy, the conception of the body as a machine from Cartesian philosophy, and experimental science from the time of the Royal Society. The book depicts the prominent roles played by such philosopher scientists as Paracelsus, Francis Bacon, René Descartes, and John Locke. The book puts special emphasis on Robert Boyle as a central figure in seventeenth century science. Boyle's health status as a patient and his scientific collaboration with numerous colleagues led to the launch of the mechanical model of the body.

The book describes the acceptance of the model by a growing research community and its application to experimental developments in medicine and surgery. Along with the great successes, some interesting difficulties about controlled trials emerged early. Short accounts demonstrate the application of the mechanical model to surgery and medicine. The book pays particular attention to how patients and experimental subjects were treated as the mechanical model was developed and increasingly accepted. By the beginning of the twentieth century the model had become the core of medical education and practice in the Western world, and mechanical patients became the norm. By mid-century, it was becoming a common place to think that mechanical health was the most significant contributor to a good life.

We are living longer, and this increased longevity was at first attributed to the success of mechanical medical science consisting of improved public health and more available medical treatment. In 1960s, Thomas McKeown—a physician and historian of medicine—opposed this view by arguing that people were living longer not because they had more access to better doctors but because they lived in improved social environments and exhibited healthier behaviors. An entire literature on the social determinants of health followed along with the beginnings of a slow movement toward a more social and relational model of health.

Just as Galenic medicine was internalized in earlier centuries, so has the idea of the mechanical patient become deeply integrated into our thinking, even though aspects of it are patently false. A good example is the notion that human beings are primarily isolated individual mechanical entities whose health can be compared to that of a smooth-running machine. This idea makes us forget that we are primarily social animals whose healthy development is dependent on close contact with other people from infancy on. Our capacity for language and most of our thoughts require interaction with others. Recent brain research and many population-based studies have substantiated the need for a more social and relational model of human health and development. They confirm that resources for health as well as for a good and happy life include such non-mechanical factors as education, a living wage, stable families, deep friendships, and loving relationships. Despite acknowledging the importance of social and relational contributors to health, we continue to be enthralled by the mechanical model. It is as if we still want to believe that we are isolated individuals whose appropriate medical care, prescribed diet, and approved exercise are virtually the only contributors to good health and even to overall happiness.

Because any successful model must become a staple of medical thinking and public policy, it will take a long time for a social/relational model of health to gain widespread acceptance. The book sketches the beginnings of such a model and indicates the need for a collective effort to accelerate its articulation and promotion.

Chapter 2

Aristotle and a Good Life

Aristotle (384–322 BC)

Figure 2.1   Aristotle.

Aristotle's conception of the world and the place of health in it was a critical contribution to Galen's medical framework and also served more generally as the philosophical foundation for medieval science until the Scientific Revolution more than 2,000 years later. His ideas about hierarchy have a powerful historical importance, and his views about the relation between health and a good life are particularly relevant to the problems we face today (Figure 2.1).

Aristotle was Plato's prize student, but he disagreed with his teacher in important ways. Unlike Plato, Aristotle believed that the physical world was stable and knowable—it was not chaotic. This made it possible to gain practical knowledge based on observation. In Raphael's painting, The School of Athens, Plato points to the heavens where true knowledge is to be found and Aristotle stretches his hand to the world around us.

Aristotle was a habitual and careful observer of nature. He identified and grouped very many animals, plants, and minerals into natural kinds, and thus provided a solid observational basis for methods of classification—many of which remain in use.

Aristotle's theories were closely tied to his observations and to the general Greek intellectual orientation of his day. For example, he accepted the four elements of the pre-Socratics: air, earth, fire, and water, and added to them the four qualities of hot, cold, dry, and wet. These ideas provided a structure for thinking about matter in general, as well as a foundation for specific areas like medicine and metallurgy. They form a metaphysical basis for Galen's humoral theory of medicine (Figure 2.2).

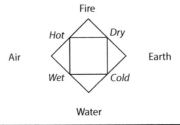

Figure 2.2   Four elements and their interactions.

Aristotle's orderly sense of the world extended to the place of humans in nature. He believed in a hierarchy of the natural world with humans at the top. All living things have something in them that makes them alive. We might call this their "life force" or their "soul." Plants only have vegetative souls that make them living things and allow them to grow, take on nourishment, and reproduce; animals have vegetative souls, but also animal souls that give them the added capacity of being able to move about and have sensations and appetites; and, finally, there are human beings with vegetative and animal souls, who also have rational souls that allow them to be conscious and engage in intellectual activity. Although there is clearly no such metaphysical hierarchy, since we now understand that all living things are equally evolved, this hierarchical view continues to powerfully affect our understanding of and our relationship with the natural world.

Politics and the state are also hierarchical like the rest of nature. People have different social levels and these social gradients carry with them different sets of resources, privileges, and responsibilities. Social status contributes to the well-being of individuals and also to the well running of the state. Aristotle recognizes that resources are increased at each upward level.

Aristotle's discussion of "goods" or resources sheds light on our understanding of the role of health in our lives. Resources, such as food and shelter, contribute to health, but health is only one of many resources that lead to the ultimate end—living well and having a good life. Along with health, education, finances, social status, friendship, and political engagement are examples of Aristotelian resources for a good life. For example, he says that, independent of health, strong friendships contribute to our resiliency in times of misfortune. Health for Aristotle is not an end in itself—it is one of many means to a good life.

In Aristotle's day, the capacity of each class to achieve well-being was different. The patrician upper class included full citizens (always male) who were educated to actively engage in the workings of the state and who possessed the material resources to live well. Middle class citizens included artisans and merchants, who were trained in their work roles, but did not fully participate in the decisions of the state. Then came foreign political prisoners who were captured in war: often, they had been patricians in their own countries and were people with great expertise that allowed them to function as doctors, teachers, or advisers. However, they had no political rights in Athens and held a lower status than its citizens. Women had even less civil status because they were not educated, could not hold property, and could not engage in political decision making. Finally, there were laborers and what Aristotle called "natural slaves," who were tied to their masters in various forms of bondage: they followed orders, did menial work, had the fewest rights and obligations, and had the least capacity to live well.

Aristotle makes it clear that a good life requires resources, and since distribution of resources largely follows levels of civil status, so does the ability to live well. He calls these resources "goods" and distinguished between three types of goods: goods of the body, goods of the soul, and external goods. Goods of the body were health, fitness, strength, and suppleness. Goods of the soul included moral virtues, intelligence, and wit. External goods consisted of wealth, property, education, and training. A person's capacities were said to depend on both external and internal goods.

Virtues are examples of such capacities, but according to Aristotle, they are not equally available to everyone. An excellent example is *munificence*, the virtue of giving very large gifts to the state, such as museums or colleges. This virtue is accessible only to those with great financial resources.

Finally, for Aristotle, living a virtuous life leads to the ultimate end of *eudaimonia*. This term has been variously translated as happiness, well-being, living a good life, or being a virtuous person. (We have a similar range of language to describe a good life: well-being, a happy life, living well, etc.)

When we apply Aristotle's account to a particular virtue—for example, courage—the goods associated with it might be presented as follows (Table 2.1).

The ways in which people use the goods at their disposal is particularly important for Aristotle. A good life for him was not a state, but an activity. He believed that living well involved action and engagement with one's social and political environment. Thus, one measure of goodness is how people behave in relation to their social context. At every level, one's actions have consequence, but those of a full citizen are the most directly consequential while those of the natural slave are the most instrumental and circumscribed. At the same time, it is possible for anyone at any level of society to act well or badly. The arena of living well is the interaction between individuals and their social context.

Aristotle did not confuse the possession of goods with a good life. The good lyre player, noted Aristotle, uses a good lyre to play well. However, he said, "[t]his makes men fancy that external goods are the cause of happiness, yet we might as well say that a brilliant performance on the lyre was to be attributed to the instrument and not the skill of the performer." The quality of the lyre is no guarantee of good playing. Similarly, being a full citizen with all the external goods provides no guarantee of a good life. Aristotle speaks mockingly of those elderly people who are timid, rapacious, and selfishly self-protective in their dotage, despite the goods they possess.

Table 2.1   Goods Related to Courage

Goods of the Body	Goods of the Soul	External Goods
Health	Intelligence	Social position
Strength	Capacity to assess risk	Training
Agility	Rationality	Right to bear arms
Endurance	Inclination to act	Possession of arms

Finally, luck also plays a part in contributing to a good life. We tend to understate the place of luck in our lives, how chance events, completely out of our control, can make a dramatic difference to the course of our lives. Good luck, for Aristotle, is not a sufficient condition for a good life because a good life must be one of active social and relational engagement, and so he argues that the absence of bad luck is a necessary condition for living well. It is nonsense to think that someone who suffers from great misfortune can still lead a good life. If one's life ends in torture and suffering, one did not live well. Aristotle concludes, "The fine man on the rack does not live well."

How Aristotle's Ideas Can Help Us Understand More about Health

This is a good time to look at how the World Health Organization (WHO) defines health. It is an example of "health imperialism." It mistakenly defines "health" as "a complete state of physical, mental, and social well-being." For Aristotle, few can have all the resources to achieve a complete state of well-being or *eudaimonia*. When I asked an audience how many felt they satisfied this account of health, a woman with multiple sclerosis argued that having a condition like multiple sclerosis does not stop one from having a sense of well-being. She argued, I think correctly, that being free from diseases is not a necessary condition for well-being. It is also not a sufficient condition. The WHO definition confuses health with well-being, perhaps for the well-intentioned purpose of making well-being the object of its efforts rather than just mechanical health. Ads from the health-care industry can perpetuate this confusion by always showing how the ill consumers of their products lead happy lives after treatment rather than merely being relieved of symptoms.

In his book *Being Mortal*, Atul Gawande notes that well-being is increasingly understood by patients as deriving from health, but well-being is often of little interest to doctors who are primarily concerned with the mechanical health of their patients. The enormous percentage of gross domestic product (GDP) spent on health-care in the developed world suggests that policy makers have also accepted this. The confusion arose due to the great successes of mechanical medicine in the twentieth century despite Aristotelian warnings. And many of us have unconsciously accepted one or another version of mechanical health as the primary resource for well-being.

In summary, Aristotle was not a health imperialist. He certainly did not think that being healthy was a sufficient condition for leading a good life. In fact, he rarely discussed the notion of health directly. Rather, he saw health as one of many resources for a good life and he recognized almost 2,500 years ago that inequalities in well-being were related to the difference in resources available to people at different social levels. Aristotle can help us disentangle our current confusion, which conflates mechanical health with well-being.

Chapter 3

Galen's Four Humors: The First Medical Model

The longest lasting medical model is widely attributed to Aelius Galenus, who is now known as Galen. He was born in AD 129 and grew up in Pergamon, an ancient Greek city in what is now the western part of Turkey some miles from the Aegean Sea. The city, which had already been an important center, was designated as a Roman metropolis by emperor Hadrian (AD 76–138) and huge construction projects created many new and massive public buildings, including a stadium, an amphitheater, and some temples. Among other resources, Pergamon already contained the largest library after the one in Alexandria as well as a temple and spa dedicated to the Greek medical god Asclepius. Galen's father, Aelius Nicon, was a well-off architect and was extremely devoted to his son. When Galen's father was told in a dream that his son would become a famous doctor, he sent Galen to the Asclepian temple for training (Figure 3.1).

Figure 3.1   Galen.

Galen (AD 129–c.210)

The medical methods at the temple are not very familiar today, but they are well-recorded—patients had been coming to Asclepian temples for cures for over 500 years. The first step was a ritual purification by priests. Patients would then make sacrifices to the god Asclepius and would spend the night in the *abaton*—the holiest and most restricted part of the temple. During the night they would communicate directly with Asclepius in their dreams. Priests would interpret these dreams to develop a cure. Patients would then sleep in a room in the temple with other patients: often these sick rooms would contain live snakes in honor of Asclepius. The temple also functioned as a spa so that patients might stay for months, even years, until their cure was complete.

When his father died, Galen had completed his studies at the temple; he was left with enough resources to travel extensively to enlarge his medical education. He travelled to the sources of knowledge in Asia Minor and, notably, to Alexandria, to study medical texts and the various approaches to treatment. At the age of 28, he returned to Pergamon to take up a post as a surgeon to gladiators, where his ability became evident—only five gladiators died during his four years there. His medical understanding improved through observation of the wounded men he treated. Like other ambitious professionals, Galen moved to Rome, which was the capital of the western world at that time. Over time, he became physician to the Roman elite. He experimented constantly and dissected many animals, but not forbidden human cadavers. He wrote extensively and became a renowned theoretician of humoral medicine. He consolidated the Hippocratic theory of humors with Aristotle's account of the place of humans in the world.

According to Galen, each person has a distinct temperament or personality and a singular place in the universe—we are all born at unique times and locations with particular propensities for health and illness. Galen distinguished four main personality types or temperaments, each related to the predominance of an identifiable humor (Figure 3.2).

Figure 3.2   Four temperaments.

Someone who is choleric tends to anger easily with a predominance of yellow bile. A melancholic personality, more withdrawn and quiet, is associated with black bile. A phlegmatic person is relaxed and easygoing. And a sanguine (from the word for blood) person is optimistic and sociable. The types could be mixed so that some people might have several tendencies associated with their personality and their predominant humors.

Temperament and physiology were considered by Galen to be interactive. Social/relational issues, like becoming angry with someone, might increase the flow of yellow bile. Also, mechanical factors, such as a particular food, might stimulate the production of yellow bile and make a person angry. To this day, we describe a person's personality as their "temperament," which for Galen was expressed in the particular balance of the four humors.

Each of the humors was connected to one of the four elements of the ancient world and with many other aspects of the world, including seasons of the year, times of life, and so on. These associations are set out in the chart below. Some of them seem familiar even today (Table 3.1).

Various versions of the figure below have been included in medical text books up to and including the nineteenth century. It shows how the four humors relate to each other (Figure 3.3).

A healthy person is someone whose four humors are in the equilibrium appropriate to that particular individual. When the humors are out of kilter, medical interventions are meant to rebalance them. Diseases can be hot or cold, wet or dry— cures prescribed hot remedies for cold diseases, wet remedies for dry diseases, and so on. However unconsciously, we still make use of these ideas when we provide "hot" chicken soup as a remedy for the common "cold." Illnesses were called "distempers" and regimens were prescribed to "temper" or

Table 3.1 The Humors

Personality Type	Sanguine	Choleric	Melancholy	Phlegmatic
Emotional affinity	Cheerfulness	Anger	Unhappiness	Calm
Humor	Blood	Yellow bile	Black bile	Phlegm
Element	Air	Fire	Earth	Water
Ambiance	Hot and wet	Hot and dry	Cold and dry	Cold and wet
Organ	Heart	Liver	Spleen	Brain
Stage of life	Childhood	Youth	Adulthood	Old age
Season	Spring	Summer	Autumn	Winter
Astronomy	Jupiter	Sun and Mars	Saturn	Moon and Venus
Astrological signs	Gemini, Libra, Aquarius	Aries. Leo, Sagittarius	Taurus, Virgo, Capricorn	Cancer, Scorpio, Pisces

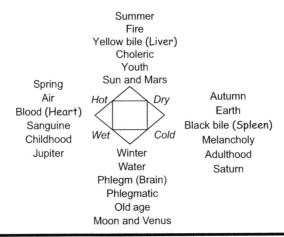

Figure 3.3   The Humors.

harmonize the humors. Many rebalancing interventions, commonly part of Galen's prescriptions for regaining health, are still prescribed today: for example, changes in climate and adjustments of lifestyle, such as diet and exercise and bed rest for moderate illnesses.

Humoral medications remain a large part of the naturopathic medicine cabinet. Other direct interventions like cupping, purges, and even bleeds continue to be used. When Gwyneth Paltrow, the movie actor, was asked about the brownish circles on her back, she declared that applying hot cups to create a vacuum and extract poisonous humors made her feel significantly better. Sir William Osler, one of the founders of modern medicine, bled patients into the twentieth century.

Galenic medicine was highly individualized. In order to balance someone's humors, it was important to know their date and time of birth. An astrological chart along with an assessment of the particular personality of a patient helped the physician identify a properly balanced set of humors for that individual. Medical astrologers provided an initial horoscope for the patient, and the physician assessed temperament and character. The link to the stars was a link to the gods who were visible in the heavens and had an impact on the health of each individual. Illness occurred when a patient's particular normal state was skewed; the physician's role was to find ways to rebalance the humors. In most cases, this occurred naturally— an illness would run its course and normalcy would reassert itself. When medical assistance was required, interventions from physicians included diet and medications to help rebalance the humors and, if necessary, more active interventions like cupping, bleeding, and purgatives were used to reduce humoral excesses.

Since the seventeenth century, it has been fashionable for scientific researchers to attack Galen for his bad medicine. Indeed, a whole book called *Bad Medicine* by David Wootton points out the outlandish practices attributed to Galenic medicine. For example, some of the dietary regimens Galen provided for his patients would kill them if sustained for six months. As far as I can tell, this suggests that compliance was as much a problem for physicians in Galen's day as it is today. We have no record of patients dying from Galen's regimens, but there is no doubt that excessive bleeding and purging harmed patients rather than helped them, especially when performed as a last resort on very ill patients.

As general practitioners know, minor conditions will eventually improve without any intervention—many diseases are time bound and heal themselves. These days, most family practice patients are the worried well. On the other hand, despite the advances of modern medicine, the course of chronic diseases remains uncertain and they often do not respond readily to the most modern treatments. So, it is not a mystery that humoral physicians, despite a clearly non-scientific theoretical frame, remained the most revered academic professionals for almost 2,000 years: their patients respected them, returned for ongoing treatment, and kept them close during the decline and death of a family member. There is no doubt that these humoral physicians helped, despite the fact that we have given up the theory that supported them.

Professional practice, for most of its history, did not depend on what we now think of as a scientific basis. Humoral medicine remained the basis of medical textbooks well into the nineteenth century. Indeed, it remains a mainstay of many alternative practices and its tenets continue to be used to treat vast numbers of patients.

The conclusion is often drawn that the effectiveness of Galenic medicine was due only to the placebo effect. This is not entirely true. Many of the medications were effective and have had thousands of years of continued use. Surgical procedures and birthing practices were developed over many generations and some continue today: bones were set, wounds were sewn up, and babies were born. There has always been a strong historical basis for much medical practice. Although modern medicine has discarded Galen's humoral theory, current practitioners still use diagnoses, implements, procedures, and medications with roots that go back to Galen and even earlier.

What is re-emerging from humoral medicine is the recognition that a person is something more than a chemical/mechanical body. "Personalized" medicine has become increasingly important. The recognition that people have different genetic make ups is only one aspect of personalized medicine. Many millions of people have already had their DNA assessed to screen for complex genetic conditions, check their parentage and ancestry, identify their genetic response to particular drugs, and so on. But personalized medicine has also come to recognize that people have differing life goals and differing social/relational requirements, which impact the kind of medical treatment they want, the kind of relationship they have with their doctors, and the kind of regimens they are prepared to follow. Individuals respond best to individualized exercise and nutritional regimens that have as much to do with their personal likes and dislikes as the state of their bodies. And individuals also have differing expectations of the results. The demand for personalized medicine has resulted in an increase in the use of naturopaths, homeopaths, and other alternative practitioners who declare themselves to be holistic and to consider the whole person in their social/relational context.

Humoral medicine was taken up by medieval Muslim, Jewish, and Christian philosophers and physicians who contrasted the limited human understanding of the physical world with divine knowledge. For them, some aspects of the underlying divine order could be revealed through human observation and reason, others emerged only through divine revelation. Only God as its creator could understand the world completely, while many aspects of it would forever remain mysterious to humans.

Chapter 4

The Renaissance and Roots of the Mechanical Patient

The Renaissance was deeply affected by the enormous health catastrophe of the Black Plague, which killed off almost half the population of Europe over a seven-year period from 1346 to 1353—recent estimates have raised the number of deaths to over 60 million. This was by far the highest mortality caused by a single epidemic in European history. The population was not replenished until after 1700.

No effective public health measures existed except to try to isolate those suffering from the plague to keep it from spreading. The traditional plague doctor wore a beak filled with lavender to keep out the foul-smelling pestilence, but no one dealt with the infected rats, which actually carried the means of contagion.

The plague had a major effect on the feudal system by increasing the value of labor and improving the lives of the fewer agricultural workers who survived. They had been tied to their masters as serfs and could now improve their standard of living because of the greater demand for their scarce services.

There were other equally devastating plagues. It is useful to compare the rate of mortality of the Black Plague to the devastation in the Americas in the fifteenth century soon after Europeans arrived bringing their diseases. The population decline in America is now estimated at about 60% of the native population: between 40 and 60 million vulnerable people who had no immunity to the diseases died of smallpox, measles, and other communicable diseases.

Paracelsus (1493–1541)

The Renaissance not only brought a new way of reading Roman and Greek medical classics, it also led to the first strong opposition to Galen. Paracelsus's revolutionary ideas about medicine and chemistry helped spark a new approach to medicine. In addition, his full name is fun to say out loud: it is Theophrastus Bombastus von Hohenheim (Figure 4.1).

Paracelsus was vehemently opposed to the medieval medical tradition. He lost his job as a municipal physician in Basel, Switzerland for burning Galenic books in the town square. He ridiculed the academic doctors of his day for blindly following useless outmoded humoral practices based on Hippocrates, Galen, and such medieval medical writers as Avicenna and Averroes. He opposed their fundamental premises and argued for a set of three elements that were critical to understanding

Figure 4.1 Paracelsus.

disease: sulfur, mercury, and salt. Unfortunately, his avowed interest in alchemy and magic meant that for a long time Paracelsus's impact on later scientific thinking was neglected. However, it became clear in the twentieth century that he exerted a major influence on the scientific practices of the seventeenth century. He is now considered to be the father of iatrochemistry—finding medical solutions through chemical cures. Paracelsus considered the body to be something like a chemical retort in which food, liquids, and air are processed into blood, muscle, and excreta. For him, a healthy person is someone in whom the necessary chemicals are present, and the appropriate chemical reactions take place. Diseases are the result of chemical imbalances or poisons. When a particular disease is identified, it is possible to test for it and apply chemical treatments.

Paracelsus traveled across Europe introducing his new chemical remedies. He is credited with prescribing mercury to reduce the side effects of syphilis—a remedy that was in use until the twentieth century. His main contribution was to originate the chemical body.

Francis Bacon (1561–1626)

Francis Bacon is one of the first modern thinkers because he proposed methods of investigation that concentrated on observation and inductive reasoning rather than logic and argument by analogy (Figure 4.2). His legal background allowed him to distinguish between "fact" and "law." He recognized the importance of empirical evidence as distinct from metaphysical speculation. For Bacon's legally trained mind, empirical knowledge was closely tied to confirmation by reliable witnesses. These ideas fertilized the seeds of the Scientific Revolution of the seventeenth century, which formed an intellectual and methodological basis for the mechanical patient. Though he did little experimentation himself, Bacon clearly valued it, and argued for the systematic collection of experimental results and other scientifically

Figure 4.2   Francis Bacon.

relevant information. He proposed a society of natural philosophers, called Solomon's House, that would collect this knowledge. Bacon's ideas were the inspiration for the Royal Society and his recommendation to collect practical information became its History of Trades project.

He expected the new science to solve all the riddles of nature. For Bacon, this would rid us of what he called "the Idols of the Tribe"—when humans tend to mythologize, exaggerate, and distort reality, rather than understand it scientifically.

Bacon believed that science should be luciferous and shed light on the secrets of nature, but also fructiferous and enable man to gather the fruits of scientific study by regaining dominion over nature. Human knowledge was no longer limited. He allowed for a very wide array of investigative procedures and extended the notion of scientific authority to include all those who could gather and disseminate valid observations. This involved connecting scientific study to the state rather than to the church. "Natural philosophers" no longer had to be clerics but could be laymen, craftsmen, like goldsmiths who had particular skills, and physicians who had collections of remedies.

His contributions to the new science have been recognized for centuries, but the extent of the influence of earlier thinkers, such as Paracelsus, on Bacon's thinking has only become clear over the last hundred years. For example, Bacon shared with Paracelsus beliefs not only in observation and experiment, but also in astrology and in the less modern notion of "natural magic." He saw this as a positive force meant to "marry Heaven and Earth" by the application of the divine to human affairs. There are secrets of nature that will allow humans to regain dominion over nature after their expulsion from Eden. The scientific leaders of Solomon's House must decide "which of these shall be published and which not, and take all an oath of secrecy for the concealing of those which we think fit to keep secret…"

Bacon also followed Paracelsus in his belief in the possible transmutation of gold and in the use of gold for the purposes of prevention of disease and prolongation of life. His writing includes recipes for making gold and for medical potions containing gold. "*Gold* is given in three Formes; Either in that, which they call *Aurum potabile;* Or in *Wine* wherein *Gold* hath beene *quenched;* Or in *Gold,* in the *Substance;* such as are *Leafe Gold,* and the *Filings of Gold.*"

Francis Bacon, like many of his contemporaries, was in somewhat delicate health because he had survived serious fevers and other more minor complaints at frequent intervals. He died at age 65 of a chill, trying to find out how long a chicken could be preserved by stuffing it with snow.

There is no doubt about Bacon's impact on the Scientific Revolution. His influence went beyond England to all of Europe, and the ideas that led toward a new science are now felt to have affected the thinking of René Descartes (1596–1650). It certainly helped Descartes to spurn previous approaches to science and to see the need for a new way of thinking that would aim for practical consequences. With language reminiscent of Bacon, Descartes claims, "it is possible to reach knowledge that will be of much utility in this life; and that instead of the speculative philosophy now taught in the schools we can find a practical one…and so make ourselves masters and possessors of nature."

Bacon's views have become more controversial in the last fifty years. In earlier interpretations, Bacon was said to assert that science would help us gain control over natural phenomena. We would then be able to use nature for human ends. But our ideas about the relationship between humans and nature have changed considerably in the last half century. Many contemporary scientists now believe that science must help us learn to live in harmony with nature rather than try to master and exploit it. In accord with this, some Bacon scholars have tried to tame his pursuit of the exploitative and interventional role of science and have slowly revised his work to focus on its more environmentally-friendly aspects.

William Harvey (1578–1657)

In many ways, William Harvey was an exemplary physician/
scientist on Bacon's model. Harvey studied in Italy and did
his early research there, benefiting from liberal dissection
practices and the newly gained understanding of anatomy.
He dissected hearts and found that the valves of the heart
worked only in one direction. His mechanical account of
circulation showed that blood circulates in the body because
the heart functions as a pump to pulsate blood through the
arteries; the blood returns to the heart through the veins. This
explanation repudiated the Galenic account of two systems
of blood: the "natural system" which was fed by the liver
and absorbed by the body, and the "vital system" in which
blood flowed from the heart, was cooled by the lungs, and
distributed heat and life to all parts of the body through the
arteries. The Galenic accounts described the function of the
organs with no clear mechanical understanding of how these
various functions were accomplished.

Harvey was a member of The Royal College of Physicians
of London that had been founded in 1518 and functioned as a
guild. Harvey's post as Physician in Charge of St. Bartholomew's
Hospital from 1609 until his death is well worth noting. While at
St. Barts, he provided free care to the poor, was Royal Physician
to King Charles I, maintained a lucrative practice to the rich,
trained medical students, and did much of his research. Harvey
is an exemplar for a long medical tradition of practicing, teaching, and doing research while caring for the poor and earning a
good living from the well-off.

St. Bartholomew's was founded in 1123. It was among the
oldest hospitals in Europe and functioned as a poorhouse as
did almost all hospitals of the time. During the Reformation,
St. Bartholomew's was defunded and then reopened by Henry
VIII as the "House of the Poore in West Smithfield in the
suburbs of the City of London of Henry VIII's Foundation"
in 1547. And in the tradition of medicine, academic doctors

like Harvey used the hospital as a research and teaching site, although there was no formal medical school there until the nineteenth century.

René Descartes (1596–1650)

René Descartes was a theoretician with a mathematical bent, not an experimentalist like Harvey. He had spent some years studying physiology and believed that with proper scientific investigation, there would emerge "clear and distinct" ideas about sickness and health, and birth and death. He went so far as to say in a letter to the Marquess of Newcastle that "the preservation of health has always been the principal end of my studies." He declared that he hoped to devise "a system of medicine which is founded on infallible demonstrations." His goal was nothing less than to create a mathematical basis for medicine "that would bring certainty to current vagaries about health and illness so that our knowledge of the nature of the body would be made precise and determinate" (Figure 4.3).

Figure 4.3   René Descartes.

Descartes believed the human body to be a clockwork mechanism. In illness, it continues to observe the mechanical laws of nature like a badly functioning clock. In his *Sixth Meditation,* for example, Descartes states: "And as a clock, composed of wheels and counter weights, observes not the less accurately all the laws of nature when it is ill made, and points out the hours incorrectly, than when it satisfies the desire of the maker in every respect; so likewise if the body of man be considered as a kind of machine, so made up and composed of bones, nerves, muscles, veins, blood, and skin, that although there were in it no mind, it would still exhibit the same motions which it at present manifests involuntarily, and therefore without the aid of the mind, [and simply by the dispositions of its organs]."

The clock metaphor was applied not only to the human body, but to the world as a whole. Later debates between Gottfried Leibniz and Isaac Newton continued this metaphor about the nature of the world. They argued about whether God as the clockmaker ever had to intervene in his creation to wind and adjust his clock.

Descartes disparaged Galen and had great hopes for a new kind of medicine. Descartes wrote:

> It is true that medicine at present contains little of such great value; but without intending to belittle it, I am sure that everyone, even among those who follow the profession, will admit that everything we know is almost nothing compared with what remains to be discovered, and that we might rid ourselves of an infinity of maladies of body as well as of mind, and perhaps also of the enfeeblement of old age, if we had sufficient understanding of the causes from which these ills arise and of all the remedies which nature has provided.

For Descartes, knowledge carries certainty—it is derived from first principles, which are themselves certain and about which there can be no doubt. He believes that this rationalist method can apply to all areas accessible to reason, including medicine. He is the originator of the idea of the mechanical patient.

Inherent in the Cartesian approach was a separation of the body from the person. For Descartes, the body is a machine that can be understood entirely apart from the person who, as it were, inhabits it. Gilbert Ryle, a twentieth century philosopher, later attacked this view of the person as "a ghost in a machine." Descartes proposes that we study the body without considering the person at all. The separation of body and mind creates a powerful effect on the relationship between physicians and patients. If a sick body is independent of the person who inhabits it, then the physician, as an expert about the body, has the principal authority to deal with disease. Because Descartes gives our bodies over to scientific medicine he turns us into "patients." And as his vision was realized, we became more passive as patients and have remained so ever since. It is only in recent years there have been small glimmers of change to humanize medicine by reintegrating the person and the body.

There is no doubt that perceiving the body as a machine was a very fruitful way of thinking about it. The approach has led to many successes in the history of medicine, from the view of the heart as a pump to the idea of the digestive tract as part of a food processing plant with plumbing spigots and drains.

Descartes has had enormous influence on investigations of the body. Research on the bio-mechanical framework flourished. Much of the experimental work of the seventeenth century was an effort to explore and better understand the mechanical body. As we shall see, Robert Boyle was most certainly influenced by Descartes's view of the mechanical body. However, his work was largely practical and experimental rather than mathematical and deductive.

Pierre-Simon Laplace (1749–1827)

In the early nineteenth century, Descartes's rationalism found its most extreme adherent in Pierre-Simon Laplace. Outdated physics and mathematics continue to influence our current thinking in the same way that Galen's humoral theory remains deeply embedded in our understanding of health. A good example of an outdated idea that persists in our current thinking is Laplace's Demon. Pierre Simon Laplace wrote in 1814 in *A Philosophical Essay on Probabilities*:

> We may regard the present state of the universe as the effect of its past and the cause of its future. An intellect which at a certain moment would know all forces that set nature in motion, and all positions of all items of which nature is composed, if this intellect were also vast enough to submit these data to analysis, it would embrace in a single formula the movements of the greatest bodies of the universe and those of the tiniest atom; for such an intellect nothing would be uncertain and the future just like the past would be present before its eyes.

This is the clearest and most deeply accepted account of rationalist mechanistic determinism that I have found. Of course, there can be no such being as the one Laplace describes. Nor do we expect to ever have such a formula because physics has passed that point. The new quantum mechanics concluded that there are many phenomena that are by their very nature unpredictable. Yet many of us still believe, without justification, that the world is deterministic and hence there can be no free will.

Although we now recognize in theory that Laplace's notion of a completely deterministic universe is not possible, it is still deeply embedded in our thinking. Much as we continue to take hot chicken soup to combat the common cold, we continue to consider that a deterministic and mechanistic account of all our actions remains feasible.

If our mechanical body is controlled entirely by forces beyond our individual control, then we must wait for medical interventions to set us straight. We must therefore rely on medical scientists who are the only ones who truly understand the laws that govern our bodies and, hence, how to repair them. The development of this view accompanied the rise of modern scientific medicine. It reached its height in the first part of the twentieth century and it remains strongly influential in practice today despite the fact that we recognize that health, and especially well-being, can be affected by many factors, including social/relational ones.

Chapter 5

Robert Boyle: The First Mechanical Patient

Robert Boyle (1627–1691)

Robert Boyle, the renowned scientist, has been largely forgotten in the usual histories of medicine despite the fact that he was, according to Michael Hunter, "arguably the most influential figure in the emerging culture of late seventeenth century Britain" and the main patron of the Scientific Revolution in England (Figure 5.1). Boyle is of particular interest for us because, during his entire active life as a scientist, he was unhealthy. Until recently his poor health has been ignored, as has the diversity of his interests. He is emerging as an important, powerful, early medical scientist who was also a patient. He, more than most other figures during the Scientific Revolution, brought together the Cartesian rationalist picture of the body as a machine with the more experimental Paracelsian view of the chemical nature of the body. After Boyle, the scientific understanding of the mechanical patient became the objective of medical research.

Figure 5.1   Robert Boyle.

Scholarly interest in Boyle was reinvigorated in the late twentieth century when his surviving papers were carefully reviewed. Boyle is the perfect person to introduce us to the growing complexity surrounding the understanding of health during the Scientific Revolution and the changing relationship between patients and scientific medicine. Boyle was not a solitary figure—he had powerful social connections to the English aristocracy, and he developed working relationships with many of the philosopher-scientists of his time, from John Locke to Robert Hooke to Isaac Newton. His very close relationship with his sister played an important personal and professional role. And finally, his serious illnesses gave him long experience as a patient.

Boyle was the youngest of seven sons among the 14 children of Richard Boyle, the first Earl of Cork (1566–1643). Richard Boyle has been described as "one of the richest and most influential men in Britain." He was probably among the first billionaires in Britain—he accumulated great wealth by leveraging his position as the Lord High Treasurer of Ireland into one of the largest landholdings in the country. He established towns on his accumulated property, built castles, hired a large private army to defend his holdings, and mined his estates for minerals to increase his income.

The elder Boyle was 61, wealthy, and titled when Robert was born in Ireland. For the first years of his life, Robert Boyle was sent to an Irish wet nurse in the country to give him a better chance at surviving infancy, and also to avoid premature emotional attachment to his aristocratic family. (Only seven of his siblings survived to adulthood.) He had very little contact with his mother, who died when he was three, and he hardly knew his father, who sent him to Eton at the age of 8. In *Aubrey's Brief Lives*, one of his school mates at Eton describes Boyle as "very sickly and pale." In 1639, when Boyle was 12, he and his brother Francis were sent on a grand tour of Europe with Isaac Marcombes as their governor and tutor. After visiting much of Europe, Boyle stayed with Marcombes until he was 16, partly because of unsettled conditions in Ireland and partly because funds for his return journey were stolen by their messenger. In 1643, while Robert was still in Europe, his father died. The elder Boyle had fallen out of favor and lost control of some of his fortune, but nonetheless left a substantial inheritance.

During a thunderstorm in Switzerland, when Boyle was 12, he had a profound religious experience that molded his religious feelings and had a lasting impact on his intellectual outlook. Throughout his life, he continually tried to integrate these deep religious beliefs with his scientific work. His scrupulous honesty in observation, his fear of oaths that could not be fulfilled, and his worry about the atheistic consequence of some scientific positions, all contributed to his complex scientific and religious thinking and his relationship with other scientist-philosophers of his day.

Boyle returned to England in 1644 at the age of 17. As an orphaned adolescent, he resumed his lifelong close relationship with his older sister Katherine Jones, Viscountess Ranelagh (1615–1691) and spent a considerable amount of time settling his share of his father's legacy and establishing himself at Stalbridge, a town-sized family estate that had been left to him. His sister was an intellectual with a special interest in medicine—she collected and published medical recipes. Katherine Jones introduced Boyle to Samuel Hartlib (c.1600–1662), the German born "intelligencer" who made his living by gathering and disseminating information about scientific practices and innovations in such diverse fields as alchemy, animal husbandry, and medicine.

Boyle and Samuel Hartlib

Hartlib was an advocate of the formal collection and documentation of all useful knowledge (pansophy). This eventually became the History of Trades project of the Royal Society—to gather practical information in all areas advocated by Bacon in *New Atlantis*. Hartlib also perpetuated Bacon's vision of a science led by natural philosophers rather than clerics. The circle surrounding Hartlib exchanged information and sought help from each other in their projects. Boyle, for example, attempted to apply some of Hartlib's modern methods of animal husbandry at his estates.

Hartlib was a follower and popularizer of Paracelsus and communicated with alchemists actively seeking individual cures. He valued the practical knowledge of working physicians and provided members of his group with medical recipes. From Hartlib, Boyle learned about chemical remedies to prevent illness, improve health, and cure disease. This strand of Boyle's interest continued throughout his life. He purchased formulae of all kinds, consulted many healthcare providers, and tried out a multitude of potential cures on himself and his family.

Much of the practical knowledge of the time consisted of closely held trade secrets: many practitioners, including physicians, kept their recipes for remedies, elixirs, and tonics to themselves because their exclusivity contributed to their livelihood. Hartlib believed that there were even deeper secrets about universal elixirs, such as the Philosopher's Stone that could cure all disease and preserve health.

Boyle corresponded frequently with Hartlib and considered his circle to be an "invisible college." Members of this group were in frequent contact with each other. It included collectors of health remedies, such as a Benjamin Worsley (1617–1677) and the Boate brothers, Gerard (1604–1650) and Arnold (1606–1653), from whom Boyle purchased numerous recipes. The group also included people interested in the new science, such as William Petty (1626–1687) who, with Boyle and others, was a founder of the Royal Society. Boyle's communication with this group almost certainly sparked his interest in alchemy and chemistry, as well as his desire to build a laboratory at Stalbridge.

By the late 1640s, Boyle had developed a keen interest in the new experimental science and gathered information that contributed to it. This included his search for the Philosopher's Stone. These facets of his beliefs and activities continued to evolve throughout his life. Until 1649, when he was 22, his writings were primarily literary and religious rather than scientific. However, he had already tried and failed to establish an alchemical laboratory to seek the Philosopher's Stone. In a letter to his sister Katherine in 1647, Boyle compared the crumbling of his metallurgical oven to the religious fragmentation of the day.

> That great furnace whose conveying hither has taken up so much of my care….has been brought to my hands crumbled into as many pieces as we into sects, and all the fine experiments and castles in the air I had built upon its safe arrival have felt the fate of their foundation. Well I see I am not designed to the finding out the Philosopher's Stone, I have been so unlucky in my first attempts in chemistry.

In 1649, Boyle contracted a case of the ague (a severe fever, now thought to be malaria) from which he almost died and from that point on he suffered ill health. He developed tremors in his hands so that he could not write, and his voice became weakened so that one had to strain to hear him. In another letter to his sister that year, written while he was recovering in Bath, he declared his acceptance of God's will.

> What [God] has decreed of me, He best knows, for my part, I shall pray for a perfect resignation to his [blessed] Will, and a resembling acquiescence in it. And I hope Spirit will so conform me to his dispensations that I may cheerfully by his assignment, either continue my work, or ascend to receive my wages.

His illness marked an important turning point: it intensified his interest in science and medicine. His first non-literary manuscript was a series of "Memorialls Philosophicall," a collection of recipes and formulae, begun in January 1650, which contained medical remedies, many of which were for fever. Some examples include the use of nutmeg and alum or cobwebs and snails for the ague, and a poultice for the feet guaranteed to cure the fever "prepared by pounding leaven, onions and garlic, and pigeon dung into a paste with turpentine." These recipes, typical of traditional herbal remedies of the day, were employed by academic doctors, as well as non-academic "empirics" (practitioners without academic training). This period also marked the beginning of Boyle's attacks on Galenic medicine. In his book, he declares that purgatives used in Galen's medicine do more harm than good.

He continued his pursuit of the good magic in alchemy and succeeded in outfitting his first laboratory in Stalbridge later in 1649. The critical piece of apparatus was another oven, one that worked and was capable of keeping a high temperature for long periods of time in order to do metallurgical experiments.

Boyle and George Starkey (1628–1665)

Soon after his illness, Boyle had his first contact with George Starkey through Robert Child (1613–1654), another member of the Hartlib circle. Starkey was an American graduate of Harvard who had trained as a physician and alchemist. Boyle first consulted Starkey about his health, but their relationship quickly evolved and Starkey introduced Boyle to the scientific fundamentals of laboratory work, alchemy, and alchemical medicine. Starkey brought together many strands of Boyle's thinking. He believed in the need for God's help in unearthing the secrets of nature, and he was a gifted experimental chemist able to test the results of these revelations. And Starkey's objectives coincided with Boyle's: to discover and make use of the Philosopher's Stone. Starkey believed with Boyle that the fruits of this labor should be disseminated to improve human well-being. Starkey also believed that the secrets of the Philosopher's Stone should be carefully guarded so that they would not be abused and converted from their "luciferous" or light-giving role into a "lucriferous" or merely commercial application for the benefit of the rich.

In his letters of 1651 and 1652, having taken Boyle into his confidence, Starkey repeatedly describes many chemical cures as the products of his alchemical work. He refers to the "Philosopher's Elixir," a universal cure for disease, and claims to have created the universal solvent, the alkahest, which reduces material to its basic constituents. In the surviving letters, it is evident that Starkey's alchemical pursuit has as its objective not merely the creation of gold but also a panacea— a cure for all ills. Starkey boasts of using the alkahest to create a special kind of sulfur (one of Paracelsus's philosophical elements) that will contribute to these objectives and tells Boyle that with it,

> *you* will clothe paupers and *I* heal the desperate
> among them. I prophesy that you will be nobler than

> van Helmont and Paracelsus himself, for whatever
> things I have found are yours, not because I solicit
> your munificence, which is very great in this, but
> from that sincere love and honour (in which I
> attend you).

Here, Starkey appears to refer to the creation of gold with
which Boyle will be able to enrich the poor while Starkey
takes for himself the use of the panacea to heal the hopelessly
ill. This passage also strongly suggests that Boyle has funded
this work through his "munificence," a philanthropic virtue
only available to the wealthy.

Boyle was an ideal virtuoso—a gentleman-scientist of the
first order. His wealth, aristocratic background, and connections to political power contributed mightily to his position in
the scientific world. Throughout his life, Boyle supported the
research efforts of many individuals: he established numerous
experimental laboratories, and he funded religious and charitable works, such as translating the bible and spreading the
gospel to other parts of the world. He purchased recipes from
healers. And he hired amanuenses (secretaries) to record his
writings, as well as "laborants" and "operators" (technicians) to
support his experimental research.

There is a lack of clarity about Starkey's relationship with
Boyle. Was he a collaborator or a paid "operator?" Starkey
viewed himself as a collaborator, but Boyle never publicly
acknowledged his scientific debt to Starkey and may very well
have thought of him as a hired technician. Boyle also did not
adhere to Starkey's demand for secrecy, transmitting much of
the material entrusted to him to other members of the Hartlib
circle. There has been some speculation about why he did not
keep Starkey's secrets. Some conclude that he must have paid
for Starkey's work and so considered him to be his operator;
others, have speculated that Boyle was trying to steal the glory
for himself; still others believe that Boyle felt a greater loyalty
to his colleagues in the invisible college, and even that the

college was itself a secret organization that would decide, on the Baconian model, what to disseminate and what to keep hidden.

Clearly, Boyle valued the results he received from Starkey and referred to them throughout his career. Starkey was instrumental in strengthening Boyle's lifelong efforts to find the Philosopher's Stone, although his contact with Boyle diminished when Boyle went to Ireland in 1652 to settle the Irish part of his father's estate. Starkey's experimental efforts continued during this time, but without Boyle's support, he amassed debts and was eventually jailed as a debtor in 1654. Letters from members of Hartlib's circle advised Boyle of Starkey's fate and may have succeeded in discrediting him, for there is so far no evidence of their further collaboration. Starkey continued his experimentation and medical practice and died of the plague while caring for patients in London during the plague year of 1665. His publications, many of them posthumous, under the pen name Eirenaeus Philalethes (a peaceful lover of truth), were circulated throughout Europe and influenced many new scientists. (Recently, Starkey's alchemical recipe for some aspects of the Philosopher's Stone turned up among Isaac Newton's papers.)

Boyle and William Petty (1623–1687)

In Ireland, between 1652 and 1654, Boyle's intensive experimental activity changed. The lack of a furnace forced him away from his alchemical work and toward the mechanical aspect of experimentation. William Petty had left England to be the physician-general of the army in Ireland. Petty was an expert at dissection and he and Boyle dissected hundreds of dogs to confirm Harvey's description of the circulation of blood and to learn more about the digestive process. The trip to Ireland secured Boyle's fortune, probably with Petty's help and Cromwell's approval. Petty assumed the role of Surveyor General of Ireland and amassed his own enormous fortune.

Boyle suffered a second severe fever in 1654, at age 27, when he fell off a horse in bad weather. This resulted in the permanent deterioration of his vision so that few manuscripts after 1654 were written in his own hand. Almost all were prepared by secretaries who would accompany him and record his dictation as he engaged in his experimental work. He never recovered his voice or the capacity to do his own writing. Such severe disabilities may have led him to see his body as something external to himself, whose limitations had to be overcome in order to engage in a very active scientific and religious life.

While recovering in 1654, he wrote to Frederick Clodius (1625–1661), Samuel Hartlib's son-in-law, who was a physician and an alchemist. He declared his unfitness to travel, asked for advice about his illness, and discussed several possible remedies, including remedies for kidney stones, which apparently was yet another ailment adding to his chronic discomfort. Boyle had an understandably increasing concern for his own health along with his interest in health-related research.

Boyle and John Wilkins (1614–1672)

In 1655, after he returned to England, Boyle moved to Oxford and joined the scientific group begun by John Wilkins at Wadham College. Although Wilkins was Oliver Cromwell's brother-in-law, he gathered around him a circle of new scientists with differing political and religious backgrounds. At Oxford, Boyle dramatically increased his level of activity. He found rooms outside the college, established laboratory spaces, hired assistants and amanuenses, and began several new experimental streams while continuing alchemical work on metals and animal studies of blood and digestion. It was in Oxford that he started the series of experiments on "the springiness of air" that would make his reputation as a leading scientific figure. He linked all his work to health so that even his experiments on air were relevant to his interest in both respiration and understanding why blood changed color once it passed through the lungs.

Boyle and Thomas Willis (1621–1675)

Boyle and Thomas Willis met through Hartlib—both had alchemical and mechanical interests. It was natural that when Boyle arrived in Oxford, Willis became one of Boyle's many collaborators. Willis had begun his studies at Oxford as a servitor—a student who paid his way by being a servant, most often to other students. He had joined the Oxford group in 1648 and spent 4 years working with Petty. Together, they performed autopsies and continued to dissect large numbers of animals. Petty was a confirmed mechanist who believed that the body was a machine and the best way to understand it was to take it apart. Willis used his alchemical training to reduce blood and other bodily fluids to their more basic Paracelsian components. Under Cromwell, his medical practice languished because of his Royalist Anglican sympathies and he was forced to apply his chemical skills as a "pisse-prophet"—a diagnostician of urine samples, which included tasting them for sweetness. Willis's practice expanded substantially after the restoration of Charles II and eventually he became one of the wealthiest practitioners in Oxfordshire. Much of this was due to his secret recipes for medications that were expensive and apparently effective. His influence followed him when he moved to London in 1667 at the request of Archbishop Sheldon. Boyle by this time was merging his chemical and mechanical understanding of the human body.

It was during the early 1650s that Thomas Willis began to study the nature of fevers with Robert Hooke as his technician. Willis had a mechanical explanation of fevers: the accelerated fermentation of the blood causes it to heat up excessively, creating more pressure in the blood vessels and also speeding up the pulse.

A similar approach is evident in Willis's conclusions after dissecting and examining many animal and human brains and nervous systems. Like Aristotle, Willis distinguishes the animal soul from the rational human soul. His anatomical work revealed the strong similarities between the brains of humans and many animals and so he concluded that the animal soul is seated in the brain and allows us and the animals to have sensations, to feel pleasure and pain, and to have desires and passions. He distinguishes the animal soul from the human rational soul, which is immaterial and immortal. Willis could thus preserve his religious views.

Health, for Willis, involved maintaining the appropriate level and type of fermentation in the different parts of the body in order to allow it to function smoothly. This could be aided by the use of chemical remedies, such as his "steel syrup," which Willis made using his own secret recipe and sold to his patients.

Boyle and Robert Hooke (1635–1703)

Willis introduced Boyle to Robert Hooke who had shown remarkable mechanical skills as his assistant. Boyle hired Hooke as a "mechanick" and this clear relationship between virtuoso and assistant is in stark contrast to the ambiguous relationship he had with Starkey. Hooke, who, like Willis, had begun his student days as a servitor—a servant to students— saw himself as "belonging to Boyle." He lived in Boyle's house and received an income from him until the early 1660s. Hooke was responsible for building and maintaining the air pump which the two used to conduct Boyle's most famous and successful series of experiments on the springiness of air. The air pump, like other significant technological innovations, had a considerable cost and opened up entirely new areas of experimentation. Boyle and Hooke used the device to perform the 43 experiments that included fresh evidence for the possible existence of a vacuum and experiments demonstrating that fire could not burn nor could animals survive without air. (Killing small birds by depriving them of air was a favorite demonstration.) This work resulted in Boyle's first major scientific publication in 1660, *New Experiments Physio-Mechanicall, Touching the Spring of the Air, and its Effects.* In the second edition, he articulated the basis for what has come to be known as Boyle's Law. This law states that under conditions of constant temperature and quantity, there is an inverse relationship between the volume and pressure for an ideal gas—the greater the pressure on a gas, the smaller the volume it will have.

In 1660, after Charles II became King, Boyle and 11 others founded the Royal Society. In 1662, it received a Royal Charter but no money, making Boyle's financial support critical to the society's survival and success. Boyle continued to fund Hooke, who moved to London and was put in charge of the Thursday demonstrations of scientific effects. He also provided the pay for Henry Oldenburg, who was appointed secretary of the Royal Society. The initial membership of 143 men included not only serious scientists, but also fashionable and influential gentlemen. Over 40 of them were trained in the law and more than 30 were members of parliament. Many men with only an amateur interest in science came on Thursdays to witness Hooke's demonstrations. Samuel Pepys was such a member, even becoming its president from 1684 to 1696. The Royal Society played a decisive role in the rise of the new science. Given the distinction that Bacon made between fact and law, members of the Royal Society came to play the vital role of reliable witnesses who could testify to the veracity of what was shown to them.

Although the formal roles of Hooke and Boyle were clear, there has been some question in recent years about the extent each contributed to the research, with an increasing appreciation of Hooke's work. The period of his close collaboration with Boyle continued until Hooke moved to London in 1662 to take up his role as the unpaid curator of experiments at the Royal Society. Hooke was eventually funded by the Royal Society (once more, largely financed by Boyle) to pursue the History of Trades project, which had been suggested by Bacon many years before and was later advocated by Samuel Hartlib. However, Hooke was so involved in collecting and demonstrating experimental effects and designing and constructing technological innovations in telescopes, microscopes, and watches, that he devoted little time to the History of Trades, which inevitably died a slow death. But Hooke did make a preliminary list of the various artists, craftsmen, and tradesmen who were to be included:

> Surveyors, miners, potters, tobacco pipe makers, glaziers, glass grinders, looking glass makers, spectacle makers, optick glass makers, makers of counterfeit pearls and precious stones, bugle makers, lamp blowers, colour makers, colour grinders, glass painters, enamellers, varnishers, colour sellers, painters, limners, picture drawers, makers of bowling stones or marbles, brick makers, tile makers, lime burners, plasterers, furnace makers, china potters, crucible makers, masons, stone cutters, sculptors, architects, crystal cutters, engravers in stones, jewelers, locksmiths, gun smiths, edge-tool makers, grinders and forgers, armourers, needle makers, tool makers, spring makers, cross-bow makers, plumbers, type founders, printers, copper smiths and founders, clock makers, mathematick instrument makers, smelters and refiners, sugar planters, tobacco planters, flax makers, lace makers, weavers, malters, millers, brewers, bakers, vintners, distillers.

It is easy to see the impossibility of collecting information about the history of trades in order to capture procedures used by skilled craftsmen, professionals, and tradesmen. Much of the "how to" knowledge is practice-based, not reducible to formulae. Many "trades" involve a long-term apprenticeship, repeating procedures until one could perform without error as well as mastering processes that are kept as trade secrets. The idea of transmitting this kind of knowledge in a written "history of trades" is not practicable. So, for example, even today, no one learns surgery except by practicing procedures under close supervision until these procedures have been perfected. No text book of surgery can substitute for this social/relational practice. The same is true for other "trades," from cooking to pottery to jewelry making.

When some years later, Hooke engaged in a lengthy, very public and nasty fight with Isaac Newton over the origin of some of Newton's ideas about the path of a falling body, Hooke never raised the issue of the extent of his own contributions to Boyle's work, where Hooke had been paid for his subordinate role (as an operator-mechanic). And despite Hooke's later estrangement from Boyle, who had become more closely associated with Newton, the dying Boyle bequeathed him his best telescope and microscope.

Boyle and Thomas Hobbes (1588–1679)

Not everyone was admitted to the Royal Society. Thomas Hobbes, for example, was excluded because of his skepticism about the role of experiment in acquiring knowledge. He was a rationalist like Descartes. During his lifetime, Hobbes's reputation rested as much on his mathematical and scientific activity as on his political philosophy. He had contact with central figures of the period: Bacon, Descartes, Harvey, and Boyle. His disagreements with Boyle about the air pump experiments are well described in *Leviathan and the Air-Pump,* by Steven Shapin and Simon Schaffer. Like Descartes, Hobbes did not believe in the possibility of a vacuum, and he argued that the air pump experiments did not constitute valid evidence against his views. The air pump could not be shown to eliminate all air from the glass container because rational arguments deduced that vacuums were impossible. His major difference with Boyle was that knowledge could not be derived from experimentation, but rather by means of deduction from evidently true first principles.

Hobbes came to Euclidean geometry late in life. He found that as he studied the theorems he could deduce significant facts about the world without resort to experiment—if one could get the correct fundamental basic principles about a subject, then one could deduce from them indubitable facts about the world. This was a very high standard for knowledge: one that Boyle's experiments did not meet. For Hobbes, Boyle's experiments were demonstrations of particular effects done with imperfect instruments for the edification of gentlemen. They did not result in any real increase in understanding of the world. Nor did Hobbes accept the authority of Boyle's peers in the Royal Society as expert witnesses testifying to the supposed knowledge gained. If the world is truly a mechanism, then it can be understood mathematically and causal connections can be deduced quickly, derived from a comprehensive mechanical theoretical frame.

Hobbes was a practiced controversialist. He knew everyone and fought with many. His attacks on Boyle were preceded by other disputes, including one with Descartes, who accused him of starting the fight only to advance his own reputation. In that case, Hobbes had presented an argument for materialism against Descartes's claim that mind and body were distinct substances. At that time, Hobbes's materialism was identified with atheism, which had a stronger emotive connotation than did the threat of communism in mid-twentieth century America.

Boyle and Arthur Coga (1631–1691)

Much, but not all of the experimentation in seventeenth century England was done with animals. In 1667, the first transfusion was performed: the blood of a sheep into a human. The patient was Arthur Coga, who had studied at Cambridge, and was said to be a bachelor of divinity. He was indigent, and was paid 20 Shillings to be a subject. He is described in a letter to Robert Boyle as "a very freakish and extravagant man.....Mr. Coga was about thirty-two years of age; that he spoke Latin well, when he was in company, which he liked, but that his brain was sometimes a little too warm."

The experiment was performed on November 23, 1667 for the Royal Society in the presence of many "spectators of quality, and four or five physicians," including Boyle, who presumably paid Coga. Coga wrote a description of his own case in Latin. When asked why he had not used the blood of some other creature, he answered, "Sanguis ovis symbolicam quandam facultatem habet cum sanguine Christi, quia Christus est agnus Dei." ("The blood of a sheep symbolizes the blood of Christ, since Christ is the Lamb of God.") Coga survived.

Boyle and John Locke (1632–1704)

John Locke met Boyle in 1660 (Figure 5.2). Unlike Boyle, he came from a middle class family, went to Westminster School a bit later than Christopher Wren and Robert Hooke, and entered Christ Church, the most prominent college in Oxford in 1652. His first year was interrupted by asthma, an illness severe enough to force him to recuperate in the country for several months that year and at various times later in his life. The university was then under the control of Puritans with mandatory attendance at two sermons a day, one of them in the very cold early morning. This exposure left him with a

Figure 5.2 John Locke.

distrust of sectarianism and a belief in a Christianity with less dogma and certainty.

Locke graduated in 1656, went on to get a Masters degree, and assumed several academic posts in Oxford. He appears to have been unsure of which path to take, but decided not to become a cleric despite deep religious feelings. In the late 1650s, he began to read medical texts, eventually becoming an academic physician. He developed an interest in the new science when he met Boyle in 1660. He was never a prominent member of the Oxford study group, but his notebooks indicate that he read Boyle's writings as they appeared and also much of Descartes, with a special interest in the latter's physics. He was a confirmed believer in Boyle's chemical/mechanical view of the human body and also in the early scientific method of careful description and the demonstration of effects before reliable witnesses.

Locke was a compulsive record keeper and much of what is known about him derives from notebooks and account books he kept throughout his life. We know what he spent to furnish his college rooms and to live from term to term. Much of his collaboration with others was to help with record keeping and writing. Locke was actively involved in several of Boyle's projects. One was to record the weather on a daily basis for many years in order to contribute to Boyle's attempts to connect weather patterns with epidemics. He also collected and categorized thousands of plants from the Oxfordshire countryside. Some of Boyle's manuscripts are written in Locke's hand. Though not an active participant in Boyle's research on respiration, Locke stayed abreast of it and wrote an unpublished paper *Respirationis Usus* on the topic.

Locke had training and experience in laboratory chemistry. In 1663 he attended a series of lectures in chemistry by Peter Stahl one of the many international chemists Boyle had brought to Oxford. In 1666, he started an alchemical laboratory with David Thomas, a medical colleague. Like Boyle, they attempted to make the alkahest, the universal alchemical solvent that is fundamental to the Philosopher's Stone. Locke jokingly wrote to Boyle that the laboratory could transmute gold from scholars' pockets into his hands.

Locke's lengthy contact with Boyle's work was instrumental in his belief that experimental scientific knowledge need not be derived mathematically from first principles as demanded by Descartes and Hobbes. He became the first of the three central empiricist philosophers followed by David Hume and George Berkeley. In fact, although he did not explicitly declare it, Locke's views are consistent with the justified true belief model of knowledge that is a basis for empirical science. According to this account, a person can be said to know something if and only if that person believes it, is justified in believing it (through experiment, for example), and it is true. We will further explore this basis for empirical knowledge in the next chapter.

Boyle and Isaac Newton (1642–1727)

In 1668, Boyle left Oxford to live with his sister Katherine in London. In 1670, he suffered a serious stroke but continued to pursue his interests. He refused to accept the presidency of the Royal Society because of his religious beliefs, but he did agree to accept a medical degree and became a physician. Towards the end of his life, Robert Boyle withdrew from society and no longer received guests. He said that he wanted to "recruit his spirits, range his papers," and prepare some important chemical investigations that he proposed to leave "as a kind of hermetic legacy to the studious disciples of that art." But he never made public what these were.

In 1689 he petitioned to repeal an act passed during the reign of Henry IV, which prohibited the alchemical transformation of other metals into gold. The relevant part of the act states "that none from henceforth should use to multiply gold or silver, or use the craft of multiplication; and if any the same do, they should now incur the pain of felony." A letter from Boyle to Christopher Kirkby on April 29, 1689 underscores his arguments:

> I still am, of opinion that the act of Henry IV has been, and whilst it still remains in force, will be, a great discouragement to the industry of skillful men which is very happily improved in this inquisitive age. And therefore, that the repealing of a law, so darkly and ambiguously penned, will much conduce to the public good, and be in particular advantageous to the counties of Cornwall and Devonshire where tin so much abounds.

Boyle, with the help of his friend and spiritual advisor, Gilbert Burnet, the influential Bishop of Salisbury, succeeded in getting a new act passed in August of that year. It required that any gold and silver produced using these new processes be deposited in the Royal Mint in the Tower of London.

When he died in 1692, Boyle left John Locke a recipe for the transmutation of gold along with a reddish brown powdery substance necessary for the process. Sir Isaac Newton, in his bequest from Boyle, received a version of the recipe but apparently not the red earth. Recently, Newton's papers

were found to include such a recipe, which was attributed to
George Starkey. In an exchange between Locke and Newton,
Newton says that he too knows of Boyle's recipe. He then
writes again and requests a sample of the red earth and
further details of the alchemical process. The correspondence
ends with a note in which Newton declares that he has not
succeeded in his alchemical quest and has become skeptical
of its possibility. We now believe that Newton suffered from
mercury poisoning, an alchemical malady.

Boyle's alchemical writings were largely omitted from his
published works, but some were kept unpublished and some
were actually discarded, presumably so as not to tarnish
his scientific reputation. The correspondence from Newton
to Locke emerged later from other sources. Over the last
25 years, with careful examination of unpublished papers,
more information, and changing perceptions of the seventeenth
century, the view of Boyle has been transformed. In earlier
accounts, his religious, alchemical, and medical interests
were subordinated to his strong scientific empiricism, and he
was portrayed as an earnest scientist with a high degree of
skepticism about alchemy. More recently, Boyle's religiosity,
his deep interest in alchemy, and his role in medical research
have been explored in greater detail. The result is that his
religious scruples, his connection to the alchemical tradition,
and its application to medicine are recognized as important in
understanding his work.

What emerges for us is that the permanently disabled
Boyle used his enormous resources to pursue all approaches
available to him to regain his health. His poor state of health
and his physical weakness in contrast to his intellectual vigor,
no doubt influenced him to accept the Cartesian separation of
body and mind. Boyle, like Descartes, saw the person as an
isolated individual mind inside a chemical/mechanical body.
He believed, like Descartes, that the body was a mechanism,
but he also held, because of his extensive experience with
dissection and chemical experimentation, that it was possible

to gain knowledge of the body through experimentation. He collected and tested many medications and also maintained laboratories to actively seek a universal cure by means of the Philosopher's Stone. His alchemical work was as deeply experimental as his physiological experiments.

His account of the human body as chemical/mechanical became the dominant view in the emerging world of scientific research, but it only became central to the education and practice of doctors towards the end of the nineteenth century. Boyle died on December 31, 1691. For our purposes it is important that he died a week after his sister Katherine, who died on December 23. At the time, it was thought that he could not remain alive without her—he was, after all, not an isolated individual mind with a chemical/mechanical body, but a person who was so closely connected to his sister that he could not bear to live his difficult life after her death.

Versions of Boyle's ideas have driven medical research for over 300 years. In sum, this view separates the body from the person who "inhabits" it and treats the body as a chemical/mechanical entity that follows universal scientific laws. It accepts the view that a healthy person inhabits a well-functioning body where the machine runs smoothly with appropriate chemicals in the right proportion. In addition, it holds that there is a cure for diseases that can be discovered by meticulous scientific experiments performed on the chemical and mechanical aspects of the body. Finally, this experimental knowledge is validated by some version of the justified true belief model of knowledge.

Chapter 6

The Story of Scurvy and the First Failed Controlled Trial

If the seventeenth century is known as the Age of the Scientific Revolution, the eighteenth marks the Age of Discovery. Ships of many nations travelled across the world for commerce, colonization, and piracy. They were fitted with cannons to protect them against their enemies and to allow them to attack rich foreign ships laden with treasure. The cannons required a large complement of men in addition to the sailing crew. Ships would often be at sea for months at a time without touching land, and provisioning for a very large crew was difficult. Hard tack, porridge, fresh water, and occasional bits of stew formed the basic ration for most seamen. The result of this diet was scurvy and a horrible death. Finding a cure for scurvy became an urgent effort of those who were committed to the ascendency of the new science and the mechanical body. Here is an account of the course of the disease–its natural history:

> The first lesions from scurvy come from bleeding and inflammation of soft tissues. Wounds don't heal because there is no production of collagen. You bleed into your joints; you bleed at the roots of all body hair, which later falls out. Your gums swell and bleed, your jaw softens, and your teeth fall out. Your eyelid linings begin to hemorrhage. Eventually your bones begin to break causing enormous pain. You bleed into your intestines and excrete terrible smelling black stool. You cough up your own blood to the point where you cannot breathe. Eventually you bleed around your brain, which compresses it. This causes vomiting, and eventually coma and death as your brain pushes into the spinal canal and crushes the brainstem.

George Anson, 1st Baron Anson (1697–1762)

Thousands of common seamen died of scurvy during long voyages of exploration, in pursuit of colonization, and especially during the naval wars of that time. In a particularly famous case, in 1740, George Anson led a flotilla of six warships with more than 1,900 men on a trip around the horn of South America to capture Lima Peru from the Spanish. He ended up travelling around the world, gaining enormous riches, but only 188 original crew members returned. Most of the deaths were due to scurvy. Anson, now rich and famous, published a best-selling account of his trip. His expedition intensified the rush not only to seek treasure, but also to find a cure for scurvy.

James Lind (1716–1794)

The traditional story of how the cure was finally discovered is largely about James Lind, a naval surgeon who performed the first recorded modern controlled trial (Figure 6.1). Today, controlled clinical trials are the gold standard of experimental, evidence-based medicine: subjects are randomly allocated to one of the different arms of the study and the results are analyzed to determine which of the treatments is most effective.

In 1747, while Lind was a 30-year-old surgeon on the HMS Salisbury, a second outbreak of scurvy occurred. He selected twelve sailors suffering from the disease and divided them into six groups of two. All were given a similar diet of "water gruel sweetened with sugar in the morning; fresh mutton broth often times for dinner, at other times boiled biscuit with sugar etc. and for supper barley and raisins, rice and currants, sago and wine or the like." He then used the following treatments

Figure 6.1   James Lind.

(quoted here in full, but reformatted with bullet points to differentiate the six groups, and with the original spelling and some clarifying terms in brackets):

- Two of these were ordered each a quart of [hard apple] cider a-day.
- Two others took twenty-five "gutts" [drops] of *elixir vitriol* [dilute sulfuric acid], three times a-day, upon an empty stomach; using a gargle strongly acidulated with it for their mouths.
- Two others took two spoonfuls of vinegar three times a-day upon an empty stomach; having their gruels and their other food well acidulated with it, as also the gargle for their mouth.
- Two of the worst patients, with the tendons of the ham rigid, (a symptom none of the rest had), were put under a course of sea-water. Of this they drank half a pint every day, and sometimes more or less as it operated, by way of gentle physic [laxative].
- Two others had each two oranges and one lemon given them every day. These they ate with greediness, at different times, upon an empty stomach. They continued but 6 days under this course, having consumed the quantity that could be spared.
- The two remaining patients, took the bigness of a nutmeg three times a-day, of an "electuary" [medicinal paste] recommended by an hospital surgeon, made of garlic, mustard seed, *rad. Raphan* [dried radish root], balsam of Peru [resin from the balsam tree] and gum myrrh; using for common drink barley-water well acidulated with tamarinds; by a decoction of which, with the addition of *cremor tartar* [potassium hydrogen tartrate], they were gently purged three or four times during the course.

The trial offered clear results. The two sailors given oranges and lemons, even though it was for only 6 days, were much improved. One of them was "appointed nurse to the rest of the sick." The results are indeed utterly clear, the conclusion overwhelming.

Lind says that the citrus fruit provided to the sick seamen was all "that could be spared." The fruit was from the supply kept for officers. Some ships, like George Anson's, returned from long voyages with their officers alive and most seamen dead because the provisions for officers contained foods that saved them, but since these foods were scarce, they were not shared with the crew, even as they became ill. The size of the crew could not allow for this and there was no understanding of the disease that would warrant this.

We might wonder about final outcomes of the two patients who were given oranges and lemons for 6 days. When they went off these rations, did the scurvy return? It is pretty certain that all the other subjects of the trial died unless the ship quickly reached shore. Did the two who responded to fresh juice also die? There is no mention of this in Lind's book.

Lind published an account of his experiment in *A Treatise of the Scurvy* in 1753. The book was very successful, translated into other languages, and widely distributed. But despite their knowledge of Lind's discovery, the British Navy only introduced fresh citrus juice to the sailor's diet in 1795. The cost of this delay was enormous: far more sailors died of scurvy than in battle. During the Seven Years' War (1756–1763), the level of death was horrific. Of the 184,893 men who were in the navy, 133,708 died "of diseases and missing," while only 1,512 were "killed in engagements and by accidents." Some historians have even argued that Britain's failed naval blockade during the American Revolutionary War was largely due to scurvy.

The delay in the implementation of Lind's results has been used extensively to illustrate and bemoan the time gap between research results and their application. It has become a standard example in literature, with different emphases on the various lessons and conclusions to be drawn from it. Herbert Spencer, the nineteenth century father of Social

Darwinism, a proto-libertarian and sometimes beloved of George Eliot, claimed that the story of scurvy demonstrated the ineffectiveness of government and its bureaucracies. More recent medical historians, like Vernon Coleman, have declared that the delay was because, "surprisingly, the Navy took no notice of Lind's results." Still others, like Jonathan Lomas, a Canadian with an interest in knowledge transfer, assert that this was an early example of continuing resistance of practitioners to apply the results of scientific research—a classic case of poor knowledge transfer.

Lind's book was a best seller for its time, translated into other languages and printed in three editions over the next 15 years. It made Lind's reputation. When the Royal Navy built an enormous hospital at Haslar devoted to treating sailors, Lind became its first director, despite the failure of his solution to be effectively implemented. He held this post honorably and continued to experiment with the sailors who came there until he retired, whereupon Lind was succeeded by his son.

The situation did not improve between the first publication of Lind's Treatise and its third and final edition in 1772. The pressure for a cure increased and sea trials continued without any clear success.

James Cook (1728–1779)

It was during this period that Captain James Cook organized his first expedition to circumnavigate the world in 1778. He demanded and received every contemporary support for the control of scurvy: ample supplies of Lind's juice, large stores of fresh and preserved fruits and vegetables, other suggested cures for scurvy, and a careful selection of crew. (We know that on some of the other voyages, crew members were often drawn from the poorest and least healthy parts of the population and at times forcibly brought on board ship.) Cook stopped as frequently as he could to "refresh" the ship and provide the men with fresh food and water.

The result was the first truly successful voyage of discovery in terms of health: no one died of scurvy, although the disease did occur when there were particularly long stretches away from shore. Cook made his reputation and received the Copley Medal from the Royal Society for his success in staving off the disease. The Copley Medal was then, and remains, a prestigious award for outstanding achievements in research in any branch of science.

John Pringle (1707–1782)

Cook's success was followed by intense scientific wrangling. Rivalrous explanations of Cook's success were led by Sir John Pringle, head of the Royal Society. Pringle reviewed the surgeon's records. He held that scurvy was a disease of digestion and that "sweet-wort" (unfermented beer) was the most effective preventive of scurvy because it fermented in the stomach and aided the digestive process. His conclusion was a major obstacle to the Navy's acceptance of other solutions and became the treatment of choice for a number of years, though it was of little value.

The scientific research establishment from Pringle's time to the early twentieth century hindered rather than helped the prevention of scurvy. Researchers and scientists, as well as clinical practitioners, transferred successful solutions from one problem area to another: *if sweet-wort helps with one problem of digestion, we should try it for scurvy, which appears also to be the same kind of problem.* These physicians and scientists were often so committed to their settled explanations and frameworks that they continued to press for wrong-headed solutions in the face of massive evidence to the contrary. The greater their authority, the more resistant they were to new ideas. Often their intransigence was positively harmful.

Pringle himself was not only President of the Royal Society, but also a recipient of the Copley Medal. He associated scurvy with rotten foods and believed in giving sailors foods such as sweet-wort. This unfermented beer was supposed to ferment in the stomach and correct the problem.

Pringle was not alone in putting obstacles in the way of a solution to the problem of scurvy. Kenneth Carpenter, in his history of the disease, tells of other prominent figures who advocated dramatically false or misleading views about scurvy. These include Sir Robert Christison (1797–1882) who was President of the British Medical Association and physician to Queen Victoria; Jean-Antoine Villemin (1827–1892) of the French Academy of Medicine; William A. Hammond (1828–1900), the U.S. Surgeon General; and even Lord Lister (1827–1912). Crucially, they did not understand the nature of a deficiency disease like scurvy.

Sir Gilbert Blane (1749–1834)

In the face of the medical establishment, progress could still be made on the policy front. Gilbert Blane, a physician from an upper-class family, joined the navy in 1781 as Physician to the Fleet. From this position, he had privileged access to the Admiral. After a short time, he wrote that scurvy "may be infallibly prevented or cured by fresh vegetables and fruit, particularly oranges, lemons or limes." His early letters to the Admiralty did not overcome the obstacle raised by the superior scientific authority of Pringle and others. However, he persevered and in 1793 instituted a test on one ship with the help of a friendly admiral. Each sailor received two-thirds of an ounce of lemon juice mixed into the daily ration of grog. The ship took 23 weeks to reach India without touching land. Several men showed some symptoms of scurvy, but those soon disappeared after an increased dose of lemon juice. By the time the ship reached Madras, no one was affected by the disease.

In 1795, soon after Blane became a Commissioner on the Board of the Sick and Wounded Sailors, the Board recommended a daily allowance of three quarters of an ounce of lemon juice as part of the daily ration. After this date, the incidence of scurvy dropped very quickly. Just as the poor health of sailors due to scurvy was thought by some historians to be a factor in the British loss during the American Revolution, their good health after the elimination of scurvy was considered to be a major factor in the British maritime victories during the Napoleonic Wars.

The puzzle about the lack application of controlled trial results to policy has a very simple solution. It becomes evident with a close reading of Lind's text. After he describes his clinical trial, Lind declares the efficacy of oranges and lemons in the treatment of scurvy but,

> as oranges and lemons are liable to spoil, and cannot be procured at every port, nor at all seasons in equal plenty and it may be inconvenient to take on board such large quantities as are necessary in ships for their preservation from this and other diseases the next thing to be proposed is the method of preserving their virtues entire for years in a convenient and small bulk. It is done in the following easy manner.

And our heart stops as Lind goes on to describe in great detail a process of heating the juice in a glazed earthen basin to almost boiling to allow the water to evaporate and produce a thick syrup (called a "rob") that can be reconstituted at sea. In this way, the "virtues of twelve dozen of lemons or oranges may be put into a quart-bottle and preserved for several years."

We now know that boiling citrus juice for many hours severely reduces the amount of Vitamin C in the resulting syrup, and the reconstituted juice significantly dilutes whatever is left. It would not, and indeed *did* not, prevent scurvy.

But this rob, rather than fresh oranges and lemons, was Lind's clear recommendation in his book. Moreover, there is good evidence that the rob was tried repeatedly with little good effect.

Throughout the rest of his life, Lind did not understand the outcome of his experiment. In later years, when he became an academic physician and the successful head of the first sailors hospital at Haslam, he continued to try a whole range of other cures for scurvy with no success. Even though Lind believed fresh orange juice was a cure for scurvy, Lind was justified in believing that fresh orange juice was a cure for scurvy (because of evidence from the trial), and it was true that fresh orange juice was a cure for scurvy, we cannot conclude that Lind *knew* that *fresh orange juice* was the cure for scurvy because he never acted on this belief.

This is a real-life counter-example to the justified true belief model of knowledge, although somewhat different from the one Edmund Gettier presented in *Analysis* in 1963.

As patients, we have learned to our dismay that there are many other cases where the conclusions of controlled trials turn out to be either ineffective or positively harmful, often because some aspects of the effect of a trial are not properly understood. This is not necessarily due to negligence, but to an inherent limitation of such trials in particular and to the justified true belief model of knowledge in general. Lind's failure to see the importance of freshness in the juice is but the first example of this limitation and it accompanies the very first trial. The structural flaw in the justified true belief model of knowledge, and controlled trials, has remained unrecognized from the very first trial and so there has been a growing attachment to the notion of "evidence-based medicine."

Of course, there can be parts of trials that are not, in fact, controlled and can have serious impact on the meaning of the results. A colleague was asked to bring the patient's perspective to the design of a particular controlled drug trial of an anti-depressant. The trial made sure that patients were not taking any prescription drugs that might interfere with the drug being studied. My colleague asked if they excluded patients who had used herbal remedies like St. John's Wort (which, for millennia people have taken for depression.) In the trial, they had ignored the effects of all herbal remedies and only excluded other prescription drugs. If my colleague was right, they could no longer claim that the results came only from their intervention. Often, it is not clear what must be controlled in the various arms of a trial. We know, for example, that many drugs prescribed for older people or pregnant women have not been tested on them, with occasionally disastrous consequences.

Outbreaks of scurvy recurred in the nineteenth century. In France, for example, where scientifically developed infant formula was substituted for mother's milk, babies developed scurvy. And scurvy broke out in the Royal Navy itself when fresh citrus juice was replaced with a version of lime juice that had been so diluted that it lost its salutary effect.

Almroth Wright (1861–1947)

Deficiency diseases were still not well understood at the beginning of the twentieth century. Prominent researchers continued to seek more clearly chemical/mechanical cures for scurvy than citrus juice. Almroth Wright, an important figure in immunology, and the founder and chief of the laboratory where penicillin was discovered, became well-known because of his discovery of a vaccine for typhus. His views were so prominent that he was considered to be an authority on many diseases including scurvy. The supplement of the Encyclopedia Britannica Eleventh Edition, published in 1911, continued to declare the uncertainty surrounding the causes of scurvy and even advocated several more "elemental" cures including those of Wright:

> The precise etiology [of scurvy] is obscure, and the modern tendency is to suspect an unknown micro-organism; on the other hand, even among the more chemical school of pathologists, it is disputed whether the cause (or *conditio sine qua non*) is the absence of certain constituents in the food, or the presence of some actual poison. Sir Almroth Wright in 1895 published his conclusions that scurvy was due to an acid intoxication. Wright has proposed giving what he terms anti-scorbutic elements (Rochelle salt, calcium chloride or lactate of sodium) instead of raw materials such as lime juice and vegetables, as being more convenient to carry on voyages.

Of course, this chemical solution was just as useless as those of the eighteenth century.

Axel Holst (1860–1931) and Theodor Frolich (1870–1947)

It took more than a century for the idea of deficiency diseases to be established. In the late nineteenth and early twentieth centuries, human and animal studies showed that diets deficient in particular nutrients could cause diseases like beriberi.

The word vitamin derives from "vital amine" and even though vitamins were not all amines, the word has stuck. Vitamin C was first isolated by two Norwegian doctors—Axel Holst and Theodor Frolich—using deprivation studies on guinea pigs, one of several animals including humans that don't manufacture their own Vitamin C. Their publication in 1907 was ignored for many years since deficiency diseases were just at the cusp of being recognized. The Nobel Prize for Vitamin C was instead awarded in 1930 to Albert Szent-Györgyi, who synthesized ascorbic acid (the chemical term for Vitamin C).

The most recent example of a Lind-like error about the conclusions of controlled trials was in the series of controlled trials that found that obesity was closely correlated with heart disease. In fact, a 1955 publication by Ancel Keys in the Journal of Clinical Epidemiology describes that correlation. Instead of looking for the causes of obesity, his subsequent research focused on finding the ingredient in the diet of obese people that could cause heart disease. The correlation between cholesterol and heart disease provided this more refined chemical/mechanical explanation. His research, therefore, identified animal fat as the source of (fat-like) cholesterol and then cholesterol as the cause of heart disease. Keys became the major supporter of government recommendations for the increase in the use of vegetable fats, like margarine in favor of butter and of vegetable shortening in favor of animal oils like lard. The result was the widespread use of margarine, palm oil, and other products containing trans-fats. It emerged some years later that there were two different kinds of cholesterol and that trans-fats are far more likely to result in bad cholesterol and heart disease. It is estimated that thousands of people died as a result of the Ancel Keys recommendations, much as how many people died of scurvy after Lind's experiment.

Ancel Keys (1904–2004)

Later, Ancel Keys and his wife became the main proponents of what Keys called the Mediterranean diet, which they developed after studying eating habits in France and its Mediterranean neighbors. His chemical/mechanical account of the diet completely ignored the different place that food and eating has in France and other Mediterranean countries. Meals are a social/relational occasion and food is eaten for tasting pleasure and social contact, as well as to fuel the mechanical engine.

It has taken just about 50 odd years to find more revealing dietary explanations for heart disease. Most major causes of population obesity are now included as relevant to heart disease. Diets of obese people with high amounts of refined sugar have been found to be just as responsible for heart disease as vegetable fat and even excess animal fat. The similarity to the Lind example is striking—the first insight was correct, but the researchers did not know it at the time.

Just as in the scurvy example, the politics of science resulted in many different arguments and positions for more than 60 years. There is even a conspiracy theory that the sugar industry bribed Ancel Keys to ignore the role of sugar in his studies of nutrition and heart disease. But it is more likely that, like Lind, he drew the wrong conclusion from the available evidence. He did not understand enough about diet or cholesterol in his early studies and falsely concluded that cholesterol, which was a form of animal fat, came primarily from foods that contained such fat. Significantly, drawing such mistaken conclusions is an inherent possibility in all controlled trials.

Chapter 7

Surgery and the Mechanical Patient

Surgery lends itself to a mechanical view of the body: its role is to repair and replace body parts. It has a history of treating the body as a machine and the patient as a mechanical object. The discussions in this chapter describe a series of highlights in the history of surgery primarily from the time of Boyle. It includes short accounts of many surgical advances, describes an early operation, considers some surgical firsts, and tells about the beginnings of the modern hospital.

The ancients had already developed specialized instruments for surgical procedures, many of which look like mechanics' tools. A large number of these instruments, described in Roman medical literature, have been preserved by the eruption of Vesuvius. They include scalpels, forceps, metal catheters, a variety of specula, surgical saws forceps, and other instruments that are still in use in modified forms. These tools of the trade have contributed to the mechanical metaphors for the human body as has the use of prosthetic replacement of body parts.

Throughout the centuries, wars and army service provided an opportunity for surgeons to develop their mechanical skills and knowledge. Individual surgeons became skilled at particular procedures and trained their apprentices to perform and improve them over generations. Amputations during war were well known but other procedures like the excision of bladder stones, and the draining of abscesses were also practiced. Surgeons adept at a particular procedure became specialized as they are today. Surgical skills advanced more rapidly after human dissection initiated the modern mechanical understanding of the body.

The development of modern surgery begins with a better understanding of human anatomy and develops through the introduction of anesthesia and antiseptic procedures. These steps led to the need for a modern hospital and at the same time deepened and confirmed the mechanical account of the body.

John Hunter (1728–1793)

After Boyle, schools of anatomy flourished. Galen, who had dissected only animals, was shown to be mistaken about the many organs which differ between humans and animals. Cadavers were bought, stolen and sold. Researchers and medical students were always at the scene of public executions to gain access to bodies immediately after death. If the body is mechanical then one body is pretty much like others: they have the same muscles, organs and bones. The unique individual in humoral medicine was gradually supplanted by the standardized mechanical patient. The aim was to gain knowledge of the mechanical body and treatments that could be turned into clear protocols.

John Hunter was one of the founders of modern surgery. He studied human anatomy with his elder brother William, developed his skills as an army surgeon during the Seven Years War, and later opened a museum of specimens and an anatomy school in his house in London. Some of the advances that emerged from human dissection included better instruments and faster procedures. The speed of procedures was critical because surgeries were performed without anesthetic. As their skills improved, surgeons separated themselves from barbers to form a Company of Surgeons in 1745. Despite advances, the lack of anesthetic and little understanding of antiseptic measures made surgery dangerous, painful and often fatal.

Fanny Burney (1772–1840)

Fanny Burney, a famous novelist of the late eighteenth and early nineteenth century, wrote about her surgery. She married Alexandre d'Arblay, a French aristocrat who had escaped the French revolution. They moved to France in 1802 after Napoleon came to power. Soon after arriving, Burney developed a terrible intermittent pain in her breast. It recurred in 1806 and became unbearable by 1811. Her physician, Antoine Dubois, called in Baron Dominique–Jean Larrey, Napoleon's surgeon, and they both decided that she needed a mastectomy. This was performed in her home on September 30, 1811. On the day of the surgery, understanding the likelihood that she would die, Burney wrote a farewell letter to her husband. Fortunately, she recovered and wrote about her experience to her elder sister Esther Burney in March of 1812.

No fewer than seven doctors were present for the operation; all were dressed in black. She had been asked to write her consent, but the procedure was not what had been described to her. She was told that it could be performed while seated in a chair, but instead they instructed her to get into her bed and ordered the room cleared of nurses and maids. "Ah, then, how did I think of My Sisters!—not one, at so dreadful an instant, at hand, to protect—adjust—and guard me." Her physician—Dubois had "tears in his Eyes."

She described having her face covered by "a cambric handker-chief" but that "It was transparent, and I saw, through it, that the Bedstead was instantly surrounded by the 7 men and my nurse. I refused to be held; but when, Bright through the cambric, I saw the glitter of polished Steel—I closed my eyes."

> When the dreadful steel was plunged into the breast—cutting through veins—arteries—flesh—nerves—I needed no injunctions not to restrain my cries. I began a scream that lasted unintermittingly during the whole time of the incision—and I almost marvel that it rings not in my Ears still! so excruciating was the agony. When the wound was made, and the instrument was withdrawn, the pain seemed undiminished, for the air that suddenly rushed into those delicate parts felt like a mass of minute but sharp and forked poniards, that were tearing the edges of the wound—but when again I felt the instrument—describing a curve—cutting against the grain, if I may so say, while the flesh resisted in a manner so forcible as to oppose and tire the hand of the operator, who was forced to change from the right to the left—then, indeed, I thought I must have expired.

After a moment or two, she opened her eyes, "again through the Cambric, I saw the hand of M. Dubois held up, while his forefinger first described a straight line from top to bottom of the breast, secondly a Cross, and thirdly a circle; intimating that the Whole was to be taken off." She sat up and protested: the pain was just in one part of the breast, why did they want to remove it all. Dubois pushed her down and she said, "I closed once more my Eyes, relinquishing all watching, all resistance, all interference, and sadly resolute to be wholly resigned." She described the removal.

At that point she thought the operation was over; however when Dubois and Larrey tried to lift the breast, the tumour stayed attached to the chest wall.

Oh no! presently the terrible cutting was renewed—
and worse than ever, to separate the bottom, the
foundation of this dreadful gland from the parts to
which it adhered. Oh Heaven!—I then felt the Knife
rackling against the breast bone—scraping it! This
performed, while I yet remained in utterly speechless
torture. Again began the scraping!—and, after this, Dr
Moreau thought he discerned a peccant attom (frag-
ments of diseased [peccant] breast tissue)—and still,
and still, M. Dubois demanded attom after attom.

Of the surgery, Burney concluded, "The evil was so profound,
the case so delicate, and the precautions necessary for preventing a return so numerous, that the operation, including the
treatment and the dressing, lasted 20 minutes! a time, for suffer-
ings so acute, that was hardly supportable." She described see-
ing her surgeon after her procedure: "I then saw my good Dr.
Larry, pale nearly as myself, his face streaked with blood, its
expression depicting grief, apprehension, and almost horror."

Here, the medical mask of objective disinterest in the
pain of the patient is absent. The difficult feelings experienced when close to a patient's pain are not hidden behind
a "professional stance." We become aware of the impact on
healthcare practitioners of being close to sickness and pain.
It is a subject worth thinking about.

Fanny Burney survived the operation and died at age 88 in
1840.

Ignaz Semmelweis (1818–1865)

Ignaz Semmelweis was a young Hungarian obstetrician who
began to teach in the Vienna Maternity Hospital in 1846. The
hospital had been founded in the late eighteenth century, and
it contained two Free Maternity Clinics for the poor. Women
received free medical and nursing care in exchange for being

part of the Clinic's training program for obstetricians and mid-wives. When Semmelweis arrived, he found that the death rate for mothers in the free ward was very high due to a disease called "childbed fever." No one knew why the incidence of this disease was so high, but there were many speculations. Most believed it was an epidemic disease caused by everything from the weather to problems with the birthing process. Semmelweis was very upset by the high death rate, and along with every-one else, had no idea about its cause. He did find one notable fact—the death rate in one of the two clinics was higher than in the other. He learned that after 1840, the First Clinic was accessible only to male medical students and the Second Clinic was visited only by young women studying to become mid-wives. He gathered data over a five-year period that confirmed the dramatic difference between the two clinics (Table 7.1). His first conclusion was that the cause of the disease was not the result of an epidemic because epidemics would not occur in only one of the wards over such a prolonged period of

Table 7.1 Annual Births, Deaths, and Mortality Rates for All Patients at the Two Clinics of the Vienna Maternity Hospital from 1841 to 1846

		First Clinic				Second Clinic		
		Births	*Deaths*	*Rate*		*Births*	*Deaths*	*Rate*
1841		3,036	237	7.7		2,442	86	3.5
1842		3,287	518	15.8		2,659	202	7.5
1843		3,060	274	8.9		2,739	164	5.9
1844		3,157	260	8.2		2,956	68	2.3
1845		3,492	241	6.8		3,241	66	2.03
1846		4,010	459	11.4		3,754	105	2.7
Total		20,042	1,989			17,791	691	
Avg.				9.92				3.38

time. He then tried changing various procedures in the First Clinic to make it more like the Second Clinic, and nothing worked. He became more and more frustrated by all the deaths. On March 2, 1847, he travelled to Venice with some friends. He wrote, "I hoped that Venetian art treasures would revive my mind and spirits which had been so seriously affected by my experiences in the maternity hospital."

When he returned to Vienna he learned that Jakob Kolletschka, the Professor of Forensic Medicine, had become ill and died after pricking his finger with a knife while performing an autopsy. The results of the autopsy convinced Semmelweis that Kolletschka had died of the same disease as the women in the maternity ward. He remembered that infants who died along with their mothers had similar symptoms, and he came to believe that they too died of the same disease. He concluded that "cadaverous particles" contaminated Kolletschka's wound and that cadaverous particles on the hands of medical students were the cause of childbed fever.

He instituted the requirement that medical students wash their hands in a chlorine solution before visiting maternity patients. The result was a precipitous drop in mortality in the First Clinic. Once he instituted hand-washing in the Second Clinic, the mortality dropped there too. He published a paper with his results and gained some followers across Europe.

But the medical establishment, led by people like Rudolph Virchow, the father of modern pathology, did not support Semmelweis' views, which were considered to be unscientific. They seemed to be based on the discredited humoral theory and more specifically the "miasma theory of disease," which argued that filth itself was the bearer of disease. Virchow was also opposed to the germ theory which was just then being introduced. At a medical conference in Speyer, Germany, in 1861, Virchow, who was by then extraordinarily influential, attacked Semmelweis' views. He claimed that local infection of the type Semmelweis described was only one type of childbed fever, but that it did not exclude the existence of the epidemic that most scientists believed in. Virchow declared that the disease could be caused by atmospheric conditions, disturbances in milk secretion, excited state of the nervous system, and other possible causes.

Virchow also had some incentive to argue against the causal relationship between autopsies followed by obstetrical examinations and childbed fever. As a pathologist he was deeply committed to the scientific value of autopsies and it was unthinkable that one of the consequences of autopsies was the unnecessary death of thousands of women. Semmelweis published a book soon after the congress in which he pointed out the fallacies in Virchow's criticisms, but to no avail. There is no doubt that Virchow's authority in medical circles prevented the recognition of the Semmelweis results until Lister showed the importance of antisepsis, and until Pasteur and Koch established the validity of germ theory.

Several years after Semmelweis' publication he became mentally ill and was confined to a lunatic asylum. He died there of gangrene after being beaten by a guard. Ignaz Semmelweis is the patron saint of hand-washing, and his story has made him one of the great heroes of surgical procedures.

The introduction of anesthesia was a major step in the creation of what we now think of as modern surgery. It began in dentistry with the use of nitrous oxide to pull teeth, and it quickly graduated to the use of ether for surgical procedures. W.T.G. Morton (1819–1868) was the dentist who anesthetized Edward Abbott in the Massachusetts General Hospital on October 16, 1846. The surgeon was John Collins Warren. The amphitheater in which the procedure was performed has been preserved and is called the Ether Dome. The introduction of anesthetic was not enough to make hospitals necessary for surgical procedures. They remained largely for the indigent. Most sick people were cared for at home and births continued to take place at home.

Joseph Lister (1827–1912)

When Joseph Lister began his practice as a surgeon there were no safeguards against bacterial infection. Operations, when performed in hospitals, were done without sterilizing procedures. Surgeons did not even wash their hands or wear clean gowns. They aired out the operating area during the lunch break, cleared out whatever remained from the morning's work and continued to operate in the afternoon. Most patients in hospitals were still charity cases.

Lister came to accept the germ theory of Louis Pasteur and began to look for a safe antiseptic. In 1865, he found that carbolic acid worked well when it was applied directly to the wound of a 7-year-old boy at the Glasgow infirmary. After publishing his results, Lister required surgeons, for whom he was responsible, to wash their hands in a solution of carbolic acid before and after surgery. He also instructed that surgical instruments be washed. Lister continued to develop antiseptic techniques for the rest of his career. He moved to London in later life, was knighted for his efforts, and is considered to be the father of modern surgery.

In retirement he was consulted on the latest antiseptic techniques when King Edward VII developed appendicitis two days before his coronation. The risk of post-operative infection was much higher than it is today, and so Lister's instructions were followed to the letter.

The operation was performed at home—an operating room was prepared in Buckingham Palace. Just after noon, the King walked into it. He had knighted his doctors before the surgery because it wouldn't do for commoners to invade his body. The operation was a success and he recovered rapidly, smoking a cigar in bed the next day. The coronation banquet food was donated to the poor who "had never eaten so well."

Wilhelm Röntgen (1845–1923)

Wilhelm Röntgen's serendipitous discovery of the X-Ray, at first called the Röntgen Ray, occurred in 1895 with a picture of his wife's ringed hand. This new technology was rapidly accepted by the medical world. The discovery was followed by the emergence of expert Röntgenologists, who take pictures as well as analyze them. The use of laboratory results and X-Ray pictures as the basis for diagnosis meant that surgeons and other doctors could know more about patients' conditions and get a clearer plan for surgical procedures.

The X-Ray machine was yet another step in consolidating the mechanical view of the body. Radiology was a service that required a hospital. The success of the mechanical model of the body demonstrated the usefulness of hospital-based research and training in the new scientific medicine.

Recent imaging innovations using computerized tomography (CT Scans), positive emission tomography (PET scans), and magnetic resonance imaging (MRI scans) provide far greater detail than simple X-Ray and are in very wide use today. In the early days of MRIs, they were employed as a general diagnostic method in the United States, but because they resulted in too many false positive indications, this use has largely been abandoned. A new medical specialty, interventional radiology, used all X-Ray technology to accomplish minimally invasive image–guided surgical procedures.

By 1890, the modern hospital was firmly in the control of doctors. The very hierarchical organization of the hospital was headed by a medical superintendent who had absolute authority over every aspect of its activity; the nurse matron was his helpmate, and the administrator, if there was one, worked as his aide. Hospitals no longer existed only for the poor. Many patients could now well afford to pay or were covered by their employers or insured.

A 1913 textbook called *The Modern Hospital* by John Hornsby, a physician, and Richard Schmidt, an architect, described in great detail every aspect of the hospital. The following plan is of the sterile operating room of the period. The design shows an operating room with skylights, special spaces for local and visiting surgeons, and many sinks and basins for assuring that everything is kept germ-free. Today, operating rooms are no longer described as germ-free, instead they claim more realistically to being "an almost sterile" environment (Figure 7.1).

Like churches and schools, healthcare facilities mark the coming of age of a community. Hospitals were social institutions as well as healthcare organizations. *The Modern Hospital*

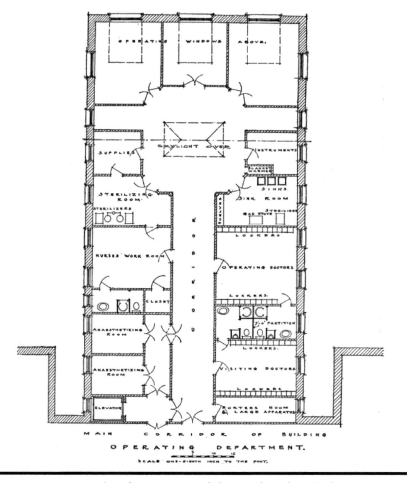

Figure 7.1   Operating department of the modern hospital.

describes three kinds of community hospitals of the time: hospitals that served only charity cases on the model of alms-houses; mixed hospitals that were community-governed and provided charitable care as well as paid care; and private hospitals that catered almost entirely to patients who could pay.

Abraham Flexner (1866–1959)

Once modern hospitals were built, scientific medicine gained more control over medical practice and the mechanical model of the patient was at its core. Surgeons, who were previously trained using an apprenticeship system, began to go to medical school along with other physicians. Medical schools discarded the Galenic tradition. In 1908, the Carnegie Foundation for the Advancement of Teaching commissioned Abraham Flexner to review the curricula of medical schools across Canada and the United States. Flexner, the son of Jewish German immigrants, was neither a physician nor a scientist, but an educational innovator. He completed the report in 1910 and made five main recommendations:

1. Reduce the number of medical schools (from 155 to 31).
2. Increase the prerequisites to enter medical training.
3. Train physicians to practice in a scientific manner and engage medical faculty in research.
4. Give medical schools control of clinical instruction in hospitals.
5. Strengthen state regulation of medical licensure.

These recommendations were a major step in the professionalization of modern doctors in the United States and Canada. Doctors would go on to create their own professional organizations, self-regulate their membership and become a very powerful voice in policy development. At the core of the curriculum was the idea of the mechanical patient.

The Mechanical Patient in the Modern Hospital

The role of patients in the modern hospital was clear: patients surrendered their bodies to the hospital for treatment. Moreover, there was no role for people close to the patient, whether family or friends. Medical decisions were made by doctors, and nursing decisions were made by nurses. Patients and their families were rarely consulted. There were no consent forms.

The Modern Hospital did not welcome visitors. The authors declare:

> We may begin with the flat argument that it would be best for all sick people if all visiting could be prohibited and it is a recognizable situation in nearly every hospital that has visiting days that the temperatures are higher at night on the visiting days than at other times, all else being equal, and this is due to the excitement caused by visitors, not alone one's own visitors but those who come to see other people... In considering the visiting question, therefore, we have two or three fundamental ideas in the foreground; one of them is that we ought to restrict visiting as much as possible and we ought in any event to limit visits to the one patient whom visitors come to see. And visits should be as short as possible.

According to the authors of *The Modern Hospital,* care for the mechanical patient is most efficiently done by those who are trained to provide it professionally and scientifically. The mechanical body should be treated in isolation from all other influences. We can see here that Boyle's account of the human body has come into full acceptance.

This extreme view of patients and their visitors was never completely implemented in hospitals, but visiting hours were severely limited especially on the free wards. The expanding role of the hospital brought with it the medicalization of increasing aspects of human lives: births and deaths moved from the home to the hospital in ever larger numbers. Fathers were not allowed to participate in the birth of their children; families had restricted visiting hours to comfort their moribund relatives.

Nurses in the Modern Hospital

A struggle between nurses and doctors was evident when the modern hospital was established. The pure chemical/mechanical patient was not universally accepted even in its early most extreme days. Modern nursing took a broader view of the patient and has done so since the early days of the modern hospital. As a result, there is some concern in *The Modern Hospital* about the nurses. The book declares:

> There seems to be something radically wrong with the trained nurse of today—the medical profession says there is something wrong; the thinking women at the head of training–schools say there is something wrong; and the lay public finds something radically wrong. Not all these elements agree as to just what the trouble is, in fact, they all seem to differ.

It goes on to claim that nurses are not sufficiently trained to perform the technical tasks associated with patients, and moreover, often have little to do except the "menial tasks" of making the patients comfortable and keeping the environment clean. The authors emphasize that a good nurse would be able to provide the technical support that doctors require for the mechanical patient.

Florence Nightingale herself argued for fresh air and clean wards to make sure the hospital environment was suitable for healing. Contemporary nurses revere her for professionalizing nursing as an art that was meant to complement medicine rather than be its appendage. At the same time, they believe that she did not take enough account of the social circumstances of patients. Twenty-first century nurses see the nurse as more aware of socio-economic factors as well as the chemical/mechanical condition of patients and bemoan the strictly chemical/mechanical straitjacket in which they do their work.

Family physicians rather than hospital doctors have taken the lead in adopting a social/relational view of medical care. Many of them have developed long term relationships with their patients and recognize the importance of such relationships. Hospital doctors continue to relate to mechanical patients, but movements are afoot to introduce what Donald Berwick calls relational medicine in which the doctor forms a relationship with the patient with a view to improving treatment. So far, these efforts have been approved by administrators but have not changed medical practice.

Lili Elbe (1882–1931)

There were many surgical advances in the twentieth century. As far as we know Lenar Magnus Andreas Wegener (who became Lili Elbe) was the first person to undergo sex reassignment surgery performed in Germany in 1930–1931. At the time German surgery was the most advanced in Europe. Of the two doctors who performed the surgical procedures, Magnus Hirschfield (1868–1935) was Jewish and a strong advocate for sexual minorities; Kurt Warnerkros, (1882–1948) later joined the Nazi party and performed forced sterilizations. (Warnerkros had some difficulties with his membership in the party because many of his patients had been Jewish.)

The story of Lili Elbe's gender reassignment was publicized and well-documented in her book *Man into Woman*. A fictionalized account, *The Danish Girl* by David Evershoff, was made into a popular movie in 2015. The variation in sexual and gender self-identification has always existed but became explicit when gender reassignment surgery became possible. The popularity of the recent movies and TV shows, and the LGBTQ movement allowed us to recognize the large variation that is possible not only in the mechanical patient, but also in the social/relational process of sexual self-identification. Much has changed since 1931.

Christiaan Barnard (1922–2001)

Transplantation that began with blood transfusions from a sheep to Arthur Coga in the seventeenth century advanced slowly until the development of blood typing, transfusion, and immunosuppressant drugs in the twentieth century. Skin and bone grafts, and kidney and liver transplants had all been accomplished by 1967—the year of the first heart transplant. Louis Washkansky was famously the first person to receive a heart transplant. Of course, the more famous person in the event was Christiaan Barnard, the surgeon who performed it. And, Denise Darvall was the donor.

Louis Washkansky was born in Lithuania and immigrated to South Africa when he was nine years old. As a young man, he was athletic. In his middle age, he became diabetic and developed serious heart disease. As his disease progressed, he was referred from one doctor to another and finally came under the care of Christiaan Barnard, a cardiac surgeon who was looking for a candidate for heart transplant. Louis Washkansky fit the bill—he was 53 years old and suffering from an incurable degenerative heart disease. Here is a conversation between them:

> Dr. Christiaan Barnard asked Louis if he would be interested in having a heart transplant, although it had never been done before.
> Louis said, "If that's the only chance, I will take it."
> Dr. Barnard said, "Don't you want to think about it?"

> Louis replied, "No, no....there's nothing to think
> about. I can't go on living like this. The way I am
> now is not living."

The details of how Denise Darvall's heart became available
are also well-documented. She and her mother were hit by a
car as they were crossing a road in Cape Town. Her mother
died instantly, and Denise Darvall suffered irreversible brain
damage. She was brought to the hospital and put on life support. Her father was asked if the hospital could use her heart
and kidney for other patients, and he quickly gave his consent
based on his appreciation of her generosity and concern for
others.

While she was on life-support her heart remained strong.
At the time, the standard for recovering organs required that
the heart stop. And when her heart stopped, it was removed
for transplant. There had been some mystery associated with
the fact that her heart suddenly stopped, but after Christiaan
Barnard died in 2001, his brother Marius revealed that Barnard
had injected potassium into her heart to paralyze it. This
allowed her to be declared dead, so that her organs could be
harvested. (Since then the criteria have changed so that the
diagnosis of brain death is a sufficient condition for harvesting
a heart for transplant. The search for clear criteria for death
continues as the point of irreversible brain death becomes
more elusive. We are not universally in agreement when irreversible death occurs.)

The transpltant operation went well, and the new heart
began to beat on its own once it was restarted. Newspapers
around the world announced the transplant and covered the
day-by-day condition of Louis Washkansky.

Barnard was very concerned about rejection of the foreign heart—had the heart been rejected, his operation would
have been a failure. To ensure this didn't happen, he gave
Washkansky especially strong drugs to suppress his immune
system. His immune response became so weak that he

contracted pneumonia and was not given antibiotics lest the heart be rejected. He died of pneumonia 18 days after the operation. It's an excellent example of "The operation was a success, but (unfortunately) the patient died." Over time, post-operative care improved considerably and now heart transplants are done routinely.

Surgical Techniques

Since the first heart transplant the advances in surgery have been rapid and often spectacular. New surgical techniques and immunosuppressant drugs increase the complexity of transplants and the kind of transplants that can be done, including multiple organ transplants, complex neurological procedures, and face transplants.

Surgical innovations in recent years, such as new and improved stents and replacement hips and knees, have given us almost miraculous surgical innovations. In 2010, Dr. Susan Mackinnon, a Canadian born doctor and a graduate of Queens University Medical School, transferred some nerves in the arms of Thomas Wachtel, a Phoenix doctor who had been in a car accident and become quadriplegic. The surgery allowed him to regain some movement in his hands. More recently brain implants tied to computerized messages to limbs are increasing this ability.

In 2011, a team of 30 surgeons gave Charla Nash a new face after she was mauled by Travis, a chimpanzee, in 2009. YouTube has a video of Nash's interview with Oprah Winfrey.

PROMs

Mechanical success has traditionally been the measure of surgical intervention; this is beginning to change. Many "successful" surgeries achieve their surgical objectives without necessarily helping achieve patients' personal objectives. In fact, the most recent measures of success are called "Patient

Reported Outcome Measures" or PROMs—a set of questions answered by patients that determine whether a surgical procedure is successful. However, the questions selected for individual PROMs so far rarely include anything about the patient's own objective in having the operation. A serious gardener who was getting older found it painful to kneel while she worked. She approached a surgeon because she very much wanted to continue gardening, and he recommended knee surgery. After the surgery she could no longer bend far enough to do her gardening, but there was much less pain. The PROMs, which asked questions about the ability to walk and the level of pain, declared the operation a success because of the pain reduction and the improved ability to walk. However, for the patient it was a dismal failure because her restricted movement did not allow her to achieve her objective—to kneel while gardening.

Such differences in perspective are not uncommon because the questions used in PROMs have so far been selected by surgeons and are based on the mechanical model and the criteria associated with it, and do not include the less clearly mechanical objectives of patients, like wanting to garden. Surgeons' criteria are about the functioning of the mechanical body, while patients' wishes often involve life goals and are social/relational. In order for patients to clarify and assert outcomes they want, it will be necessary to go beyond the boundaries of the mechanical model.

Chapter 8

Medicine and the Chemical Patient

The chemical/mechanical model of the body led not only to improvements in surgery, but also to the development of drugs that both prevented and treated disease. Over time the chemically active components of many of the ancient herbal remedies were derived and new more effective drugs produced. Much of the chemical history of medicine from the seventeenth century onward is about identifying the cause, and very often the chemical cure for disease. Today infectious diseases are no longer the primary cause of death in developed countries.

Lady Mary Wortley Montagu (1689–1762)

Since antiquity, smallpox, one of the most common infectious diseases, killed thousands in recurring epidemics. The disease was known as early as ancient Egypt. In the seventeenth century, Thomas Sydenham, a famous physician and colleague of Locke and Boyle, went so far as to claim that smallpox was best understood as a disease of passage: once you got it and survived, there was no chance of getting it again. We are startled at his equanimity because the disease resulted in such high mortality rates. In the seventeenth and throughout the eighteenth centuries, about 60% of the population were stricken and 20% died of smallpox.

One of the disadvantages of living in cities was that infectious diseases spread more quickly, and one of the advantages was that if you survived them your immunity increased. When Europeans came to the Americas and Australia, smallpox and other diseases they brought with them killed many millions of indigenous people who lacked immunity to them. In some cases, 90% of the indigenous population died through naturally spread infection, and in others they were given smallpox-contaminated blankets.

Lady Mary Wortley Montagu is one of the very few women mentioned in most medical histories. As the wife of the ambassador to the Ottoman Empire she observed how the Turks inoculated people to cause a mild form of smallpox and produce immunity. The procedure was discovered much earlier and brought to Turkey by Circassian traders, who followed the "cure like with like" rule that goes back to Galen and continues today with medical vaccines, and more extremely in homeopathy. In Europe it was called "variolation" after "variola," the Latin name of the disease. The procedure of variolation was performed by rubbing powdered smallpox scabs on a superficial scratch, or injecting fluid from a smallpox pustule.

Lady Wortley-Montagu contracted smallpox in 1715 and bore its scars. She had her son Edward variolated in Turkey. When she returned to England and a smallpox epidemic started in 1721 she asked her doctor, Charles Maitland, to variolate her young daughter. Maitland tested the procedure by variolating six prisoners and infecting them with a mild version of smallpox. None of them contracted the more virulent smallpox. Variolation was taken up by royal families across Europe but not by the general public.

Despite the introduction of variolation, there was still very little understanding of the nature of infectious diseases. Variolation was not an entirely safe procedure because one did contract a mild version of smallpox: about one in every hundred people who were variolated died of the disease—a much lower percentage than the 20% who died of smallpox.

Edward Jenner (1749–1823)

It was not until the very end of the eighteenth century that Edward Jenner injected James Phipps with the pus from cowpox blisters. Jenner became aware that milkmaids appeared to be immune to smallpox. He wanted to see if smallpox could be prevented when patients were infected with cowpox. He tried it on James Phipps, the healthy 8-year-old son of his gardener. Phipps became mildly sick from the cowpox. He was then exposed to smallpox pus through variolation on two separate occasions but did not become ill. He was number 17 of 23 people whose successful vaccinations are described in Jenner's paper.

About this experiment we know quite a lot. We know who James Phipps was. We know that Sarah Nelmes was the milkmaid whose cowpox pus was used. And we even know the name of the cow: Blossom. And Blossom's hide now hangs in the St. George's Medical School library to commemorate the great event. The term vaccinate was originated by Jenner. It comes from the Latin word *vacca* for "cow."

Today we see that the experiment was not ethical by modern standards. No proper consent was requested or given; the child was exposed to smallpox on several occasions without even knowing it. Edward Jenner was more than likely aware of all this: he showed his gratitude by providing the adult James

Phipps with free lodging for life in one of the houses on his property; James is also known to have attended Jenner's funeral.

Jenner's experiment demonstrated that the vaccine was less dangerous than variolation because its side effects were mild. Only one in a million people die because of vaccination against smallpox, while one in a hundred died from variolation. Secondly, he showed that vaccination was effective in preventing smallpox: when he exposed his experimental subjects to the disease they did not become sick at all. Nonetheless the public remained skeptical—at least for a while. It was only in 1853 that smallpox vaccination became compulsory in England.

However, infectious diseases continued to be the major killers; most people died of one infectious disease or another. In the nineteenth century, poor drinking water brought epidemics of cholera, which previously only occurred in India, to the United Kingdom and Europe. Extremely crowded living quarters increased the rate of tuberculosis, and smallpox continued to kill large numbers of people.

Louis Pasteur (1822–1895)

As a professor at the University of Strasbourg in 1848, Louis Pasteur (Figure 8.1) researched the process of fermentation. His early work demonstrated that microorganisms caused fermentation. He married Marie Laurent in 1849 and they had five children, three of whom died of typhoid fever. Personal tragedy as well as his early work in fermentation no doubt influenced his interest in germ theory as applied to the cause and prevention of diseases.

Pasteur was particularly adept at being newsworthy: he advertised his experiments to make them public and commercialized the results. He was generous to his predecessors: his work on germ theory turned Semmelweis from a poor lunatic into a heroic scientific figure. He also made the term "vaccine" generic in honor of Jenner's work with cowpox.

Figure 8.1   Louis Pasteur.

Among his accomplishments he showed that microorganisms were responsible for the spoilage of milk, wine, and other beverages, and that heating them to a temperature of over 60°C would kill most bacteria and prevent early decay. He patented the process as "pasteurization." It was initially meant to be used on wine. Many kosher wines are still pasteurized.

Pasteur ran a sensational public anthrax experiment when he injected 25 sheep with the anthrax vaccine and left a control group unvaccinated. Twenty days later he injected both groups with live anthrax bacteria. All the non-vaccinated animals died, while the vaccinated sheep survived. Extensive newspaper coverage evoked a huge public reaction.

Pasteur's work on germ-caused diseases led to the development of vaccines not only for anthrax, but also for rabies and other diseases. The first person to receive the rabies vaccine was Joseph Meister a 9-year-old boy severely bitten by a dog. Pasteur, although not a physician, decided to treat the boy with untested rabies vaccine he had developed. The boy did not get rabies. Meister stayed connected to Pasteur as the caretaker of his Institute, a connection reminiscent of the relationship between James Phipps and Edward Jenner.

Robert Koch (1843–1910), Ferdinand Cohn (1829–1898), and Maurice Hilleman (1919–2005)

Along with Pasteur, Robert Koch and Ferdinand Cohn were principal contributors to the establishment of the germ theory of disease. The superior quality of German laboratories and equipment enabled Koch's careful and extensive work on anthrax, tuberculosis and other diseases. It also supported Cohn's many years of effort to identify and categorize microorganisms. Both are considered to be among the founding fathers of microbiology and bacteriology; their efforts led to the development of numerous vaccines.

Finding new vaccines became a scientific race continuing into the twentieth century. The champion so far is Maurice Ralph Hilleman. He developed eight of the fourteen vaccines that are routinely recommended: measles, mumps, hepatitis A, hepatitis B, chicken pox, meningitis, pneumonia and Hib (haemophilus influenza bacteria).

Hillman was employed by Merck & Co., one of the many emerging pharmaceutical companies that introduced new medications. Merck began as an apothecary shop and found the active chemical ingredients of herbal remedies to create new marketable drugs for the chemical body. Other large pharmaceutical companies began as manufacturers of chemicals, and gradually introduced pharmaceutical products. Many of the drugs they created still exist. Among the most famous is aspirin created by the Bayer Dye Chemical Company. It remains the most widely used medication, and has a very long history beginning with prehistoric willow bark.

Mary Mallon (Typhoid Mary) (1869–1938)

Not all famous patients of infectious diseases were passive and receptive. Typhoid Mary, whose real name was Mary Mallon, has been described as everything from an ignorant carrier of disease to a malevolent murderer of hundreds of people. In 1906, she appeared to be a perfectly healthy woman who had taken a job as a cook for a well-off family vacationing in a rental house in Oyster Bay, Long Island. Within several weeks, six members of the household contracted typhoid fever: three family members, the gardener, and two maids. Mary Mallon stopped working there soon after the typhoid outbreak.

The owner of the house worried that his house would no longer be rentable, hired investigators to determine the cause of the outbreak. None were successful until he found George Soper, a civil engineer, who had experience in tracking typhoid outbreaks. Soper thought Mary Mallon might be responsible and began to investigate where she had previously worked. He discovered that typhoid outbreaks had followed her as she changed jobs between 1900 and 1906. One young girl had died of the disease.

In March of 1907, Soper finally found Mary Mallon who was once more working as a cook. When he tried to approach her to see if she was infected with the typhoid bacteria, she reacted violently. He called in the Public Health Department, but she once again refused to listen to their explanations and rejected their requests for samples of her blood, stool, and urine. The police were called in to capture her by force. They brought her in an ambulance to a hospital in New York where samples were taken. Her stool tested positive for typhoid bacilli. Because she was a public health hazard, she was removed from her home and placed in isolation without trial.

Mary Mallon became the famous patient known as Typhoid Mary during this period. She sued the Public Health Department for her release, claiming that she was healthy, and they had no right to detain her without trial. According to the laws of New York State, the public health department had the right to isolate the cause of infectious diseases, like typhoid fever:

> The board of health shall use all reasonable means for ascertaining the existence and cause of disease or peril to life or health, and for averting the same, throughout the city (Section 1169).
>
> Said board may remove or cause to be removed to (a) proper place to be by it designated, any person sick with any contagious, pestilential or infectious disease; shall have exclusive charge and control of the hospitals for the treatment of such cases (Section 1170).[6]

In 1910, a new Director of Public Health offered to release Mary Mallon from her confinement if she would agree not to work as a cook and to take precautions when she was in contact with other people so as not to infect them. She agreed and was released. She found work as a laundress and soon disappeared once more.

It is not clear if Typhoid Mary understood that she was a healthy carrier of a deadly disease. She was an Irish immigrant who lived and worked in the service class. It was more common to give orders to people like her than to attempt to explain things. It is also not clear that she tried to abide by the conditions set for her release. Working as a laundress or a maid paid substantially less than working as a cook. And after several service jobs she returned to her original occupation working as a cook. In January 1915, twenty-five people contracted typhoid fever at the Sloane Maternity Hospital in Manhattan. Two people died. It turned out that Mary Mallon had changed her name and was working as a cook in that hospital.

This time there was no public sympathy for her, and she was sent to North Brother Island where she lived for the rest of her life. She died in 1938. There are estimates that as many as several hundred people died because of her, but there remains no clear agreement about whether she understood that she was infecting and killing them.

Charles Best (1899–1978), Sir Frederick Banting (1891–1941), and James Collip (1892–1965)

As hospitals and universities established laboratories for testing patients and doing research, more medical breakthroughs occurred. Almost magic chemical cures consisted not only of vaccines, but also of other life-saving drugs. In 1921 insulin was isolated in a laboratory at the University of Toronto and used to treat Leonard Thompson, a 14-year-old boy. He survived to age 28. The group responsible included Frederick Banting, Charles Best, James Collip, and John Macleod. In his 1923 Nobel lecture Banting, who was only 32 years old said, "With the relief of the symptoms of his disease, and with the increased strength and vigor resulting from the increased diet, *the pessimistic, melancholy diabetic becomes optimistic and cheerful.* Insulin is not a cure for diabetes; it is a treatment."

The treatment of diabetes meant that insulin had to be taken for life. Until the introduction of insulin, medications were a response to the acute symptoms of diseases that would eventually be cured and health restored. Now there was a drug that could control a chronic condition but not cure it. This changed the nature and scope of the pharmaceutical industry: it began to provide drugs taken daily for the life of the patient to control chronic conditions.

The Tuskegee Syphilis Study (1932–1972) and Ethics

In 1932 in order to understand the natural course of syphilis, the United States Public Health Service began an experiment that lasted until well after the Nuremberg trials. This was done in the spirit of Thomas Sydenham, who believed that diseases were natural, much like other living things, and had a beginning, middle, and an end. A good part of understanding a disease was to learn its natural history. (The rather horrific natural course of scurvy is a good example.) Although much was known about syphilis, there had so far not been such a study.

About 600 impoverished African American sharecroppers were enrolled in the study. Among them were almost 400 men with syphilis. They were given some meals and free medical care in return for being in the study. The men with syphilis were never told of their condition and were not treated for it even though effective treatments were well-known at the time. In fact, one of the medications, Salvarsan was called "the magic bullet"—a modern version of the Philosopher's Stone—and was an early "blockbuster drug" and widely distributed until antibiotics became the cure of choice.

Although complaints about the study were made years earlier, the study was not stopped until an article about it appeared in The New York Times in July of 1972. In the United States, a National Commission for the Protection of Human Subjects of Biomedical and Behavioral Research was established in 1974 to develop bioethics policy. In 1979, it issued the Belmont Report that proposed "ethical principles and guidelines for protection of human subjects of biomedical and behavioral research."

Since that time, medical ethics has become a critical part of health research. However, it was never clear what role patients themselves had in establishing ethical guidelines for enrolling subjects. President Bill Clinton apologized to the last survivors of the Tuskegee experiment in 1997.

Gerhard Domagk (1895–1964)

The first antibiotics were the sulfonamide drugs developed in Germany shortly before World War II. A team of researchers at Bayer Pharmaceuticals thought that coal tar dyes could become the basis of drugs to fight bacterial infections, and the research team, led by Gerhard Domagk, found that a particular red dye had strong anti-bacterial properties. The drug that resulted was Prontosil patented in 1935 and proved to be particularly effective in treating childbirth fever. Sulfonamides were the first anti-bacterial drugs, eventually replaced by antibiotics, which were more effective and produced fewer side effects. The Nazi government would not allow Domagk to receive the Nobel Prize.

Alexander Fleming (1881–1955), Howard Florey (1898–1968), and Ernst Chain (1906–1979)

Alexander Fleming had discovered penicillin before the sulfonamides were developed. He cultured a fungus that produced it but found it difficult to grow in mold and isolate the antibiotic agent. By 1940, he had stopped trying. His work was taken up again by Howard Florey and Ernst Chain who led the efforts to isolate and mass produce penicillin. Chain had left Nazi Germany, and at first complained about the poor quality of equipment he found in England compared to the more advanced laboratories in Germany. But he persevered along with his colleagues. By 1941, large scale production had begun and by 1944 there was enough penicillin to serve all the allied forces. The three lead scientists were given the Nobel Prize in 1945. The people who participated in the trials remain anonymous.

The introduction of penicillin was the Philosopher's Stone that marked the coming of age of modern medicine. Antibiotics saved innumerable lives quickly and effectively by ridding the body of bacterial infections. Medical care was transformed. Rather than wait for diseases to run their course or vaccinate to prevent them, penicillin was the true beginning of the possibility of a cure. Penicillin also marked the coming of age of a very effective and powerful pharmaceutical industry.

Henrietta Lacks (1920–1951)

Henrietta Lacks is perhaps the most widely distributed patient in the history of the world. Her cancerous cells are everywhere—more than 50 metric tons of them have been grown in laboratories around the world and some have even been sent into space. In contrast to the biblical Eve, she has gained a kind of physical immortality.

Henrietta Lacks was diagnosed with cancer in 1951 and the malignant cells from her biopsy were so robust that they could be grown in laboratories. Consequently, her cells were used as laboratory material for the study of virology and were cultured and widely distributed. No one had asked her permission for the use of her cells in research. Her cells thrived while she died of cancer within eight months of diagnosis. The cells, called "HeLa cells," have been used in research for over 65 years.

At the time of her death, her cells were so well known that a lab assistant at her autopsy was surprised the cells belonged to a real person. No effort was made to inform her family about these still living cells until a few decades later. Henrietta Lacks was a black woman who was being cared for as a free patient at Johns Hopkins, the major teaching hospital in Baltimore Maryland. For centuries, patients like her were given care, but at the same time, were used as clinical material for scientific research. A tacit agreement was assumed by patients to accept their research role in exchange for their hospital stay. In such circumstances, patients did not make decisions about their care or about the use of materials taken from their bodies.

In 1973, Henrietta Lacks' family was told about the use of her cells, not because anyone thought they had a right to the information, but because geneticists wanted cells from her living relatives to do more research. Her family had to assimilate this pretty significant fact about their mother. Of course, there was nothing that could be done to curtail the distribution of HeLa cells, nor is it clear that anyone wanted to. But her family had strong feelings about being exploited by the healthcare system and remained suspicious of contact with it. Some members of her family wanted more information about what had happened to her cells, others wanted some compensation, but they were largely ignored.

In the early twenty-first century, a graduate student named Rebecca Skloot became interested in the origin of the HeLa cells and contacted the family. Despite their initial reluctance, she gained their confidence over time. In 2010, she published *The Immortal Life of Henrietta Lacks* to introduce readers to the living person who generated the cells, and to provide an overview of the political and scientific context in which she had lived and died.

There have been more than 75,000 studies using HeLa cells. Many of them are important contributions to cell biology, the development of new vaccines, and, of course, cancer research. Scientists at the European Biology Laboratory sequenced the genome of the HeLa cells. In order to complete their studies, they needed cells of living members of the family, which they were given. When the results were publicly posted on the internet, the Lacks family complained to the National Institutes of Health about this intrusion into their privacy. An agreement was reached to restrict access to the results of this and other similar studies. But there was no agreement to give the Lacks family any benefit from the commercial products developed from research on the HeLa genome.

To give you an idea of what they have not received, the legatees of A.A. Milne (1882–1956) continued receiving royalties from *Winnie the Pooh*, well after his death, although they did not write any of his books and most of them had never met him. On March 4, 2001, Walt Disney paid an estimated $340–350 million for rights to the Milne royalty stream. The copyright was supposed to end in 2006, 50 years after his death, but it was extended it until 2026. The Disney Corporation has been very adept at extending copyright protection: as Mickey Mouse ages, the rights to his persona remain in the hands only of Disney. Whenever there is an end in sight, Disney extends the copyright. The often-changed Copyright Extension Act is called "the Mickey Mouse Act." According to the US Constitution, copyright cannot be extended forever, but it has been suggested that it will be extended for "Forever Less a Day." One would imagine that the commercial consequences of the HeLa cell are not dissimilar in scale. Unlike Mickey Mouse and Winnie the Pooh, patients continue to be a free good. In the United States, the biopharmaceutical sector contributes $1.2 trillion to the economy compared to the entertainment sector, which accounts for $600 billion, so money is not the issue.

Ali Maow Maalin (1954–2013)

The complete eradication of smallpox marks the ultimate success of the germ theory. Ali Maow Maalin was the last person to suffer from naturally occurring smallpox. He was treated in Somalia in 1977 and fully recovered. He died in 2013. Although infectious diseases have continued to kill people in the developing world, large plagues of infectious diseases, like smallpox, had diminished significantly and had stopped being the major causes of death in the twentieth century. Large scale vaccination programs contained many of the most virulent diseases, and better living conditions reduced the incidence of others.

Sam Wagstaff (1921–1987) and Robert Mapplethorpe (1946–1989)

HIV is a relatively new infectious disease that spread after smallpox was eradicated. It has had devastating consequences in large parts of the world, especially in south Saharan Africa. The management of the disease is now accomplished by using different antiretroviral medications, which maintain the immune system and reduce the incidence of infections. The effect has been, at least in the developed world, to convert HIV infection into a chronic disease.

In the 1980s, the HIV/AIDS epidemic mobilized the gay community to struggle for the improved treatment of AIDS patients many of whom were gay men. The organizations that were created fought for increased participation of patients in their care, better treatment, and more end of life support. During his life Robert Mapplethorpe became one of the prominent figures whose work celebrated the gay community. He and his partner Sam Wagstaff died of AIDS about a year apart. The increasing acceptance of gay men, lesbian women, bisexual men and women, and transsexuals accelerated during the height of the HIV/AIDS epidemic. Their influence and participation in their medical treatment served as a forerunner of the current change in the patient role in medicine and healthcare. The Mapplethorpe Foundation has raised large amounts of money not only to preserve Mapplethorpe's photographic legacy, but also to fund AIDS research.

HIV/AIDS is different from most historical epidemics where death occurred relatively quickly after the onset. Although there is still no vaccine for it, HIV/AIDS is now treated as a chronic disease, which can be contained by antiretroviral drugs. As a result, the life expectancy of a 20-year-old newly infected by HIV but who immediately begins antiretroviral therapy is estimated to be 70. The average life expectancy for HIV positive men on antiretroviral therapy is 62, and of HIV positive women it is 64. The annual cost per patient for antiretroviral drugs is about $20,000 in developed countries.

WHO Atlas

In 2014, the World Health Organization published an Atlas of Non-Communicable Diseases Profiles of countries around the world. It showed that in the industrialized world about 90% of deaths were due to non-communicable chronic diseases led by heart disease and cancer. The data from Canada, the US, and the UK are shown in Table 8.1. These diseases have slow

Table 8.1   WHO Mortality Atlas: Causes of Death 2014

Country	Injuries %	Communicable Diseases %	Cardiovascular Disease %	Cancers %	Chronic Respiratory Diseases %	Diabetes and Other NCDs %	All NCDs %
Central African republic	7	73	8	3	2	7	20
Kenya	10	64	8	7	1	10	25
Uganda	13	60	9	5	2	11	27
Canada	6	5	27	30	7	25	89
United Kingdom	4	7	31	29	8	21	89
United States	6	6	31	23	8	26	88

Source: Date taken from WHO (2014).

onset and lingering effects before they become acute. The percentage of deaths due to communicable diseases of all kinds, including HIV/AIDS, is between 6% and 8%—almost the same as death from injuries including car accidents, suicides and homicides. Developed countries are very different from developing ones, of which Central African Republic, Kenya and Uganda are examples. There, the majority of deaths continue to be caused by communicable diseases, which have very clear causes, abrupt onsets, and are often accompanied by acute symptoms that demand specific treatment.

In the developed world we no longer die in our sixties of heart attacks, lung cancer, and strokes as did our parents and grandparents in the mid-twentieth century. Chronic diseases like cancer, heart disease, and type 2 diabetes begin later and last longer than ever. One way to distinguish ourselves from people who lived even further back in the seventeenth century is that we not only have greater longevity at birth, but that the age at which people acquire chronic diseases has risen from 40 to 65. As a result, we have 25 more years of mature good health for much of our population, but we also have a much longer period of suffering from chronic disease. In a New Yorker cartoon one man says to another, "The trouble with extending life is that it all happens at the end."

A major issue in the developed world became the detection and management of early stages of chronic disease. A system centered on hospitals is well equipped to deal with acute episodes of disease, but poorly organized to respond to the onset of long term chronic conditions. The pharmaceutical industry recognized this change very early on and has produced an enormous variety of medications to respond to chronic diseases of every kind and at ever earlier stages. The threshold for disease has been lowered continually for an expanding collection of patients. "Blockbuster" drugs like statins are taken by very many people for a very long time. As a result, the pharmaceutical industry now takes a larger proportion of the healthcare dollar and plays a major role in national economies. In its ads it promises that the drugs will deliver well-being, not merely health, if we ignore the side effects in small print. The chemical aspect of the mechanical model has been an enormous success for the companies that produce chemicals for an increasing population of patients diagnosed with very early stages of chronic conditions.

The chemical response to chronic disease has resulted in an increased interest in dealing with chronic conditions that do not rely primarily on chemicals. This approach depends on weakening the influence of the chemical/mechanical model of the patient. There is good, increasing evidence to show that many chronic conditions are correlated with a wide variety of social/relational factors, many of them outside the parameters of the chemical/mechanical aspects of the patient, but it has so far proved difficult to change the medical research agenda to include them.

Brenda Zimmermann (1956–2014)

A less mechanical account of chronic disease was suggested by making a distinction between simple, complicated, and complex projects. While the acute phase of chronic disease is complicated, the origin of such diseases is far more complex and includes many social and relational factors. Here is the most recent version of a distinction I originally made together with Brenda Zimmermann between three kinds of projects ones that were simple, complicated, and complex (Table 8.2).

These ideas apply very well to the distinction between managing acute and chronic diseases (Table 8.3).

In January of 2018, the New England Journal of Medicine published "Patient Engagement Survey: Social Networks to Improve Patient Health." The survey asked health care executives, clinical leaders, and clinicians for the three most significant impacts of social networks on health. The results are in the Table 8.4.

Table 8.2 Simple Complicated and Complex Projects

Simple Projects	Complicated Projects	Complex Projects
Following a Recipe	Sending a Rocket to the Moon	Raising a Second Child
The Recipe is essential Recipes are tested to assure replicability No particular expertise is needed; knowing how to cook increases success Recipes produce standard products Certainty of same results every time Optimism re results	Formulae are critical and necessary Sending one rocket increases assurance that the next will be OK High level of expertise in many fields and coordination Rockets are similar in critical ways High degree of certainty of outcome Optimism re results	Formulae have only a limited application Raising one child gives no assurance of success with the next Expertise can help but is not sufficient Every child is unique in many ways Uncertainty of outcome remains Optimism re results

Table 8.3 Complicated Acute Diseases and Complex Chronic Diseases

Complicated Acute Diseases	Complex Chronic Diseases
• Abrupt onset • Often all causes can be identified and measured • Diagnosis and prognosis are often accurate • Specific therapy or treatment is often available • Protocol-based intervention is usually effective: cure is likely with return to normal health • Professionals are knowledgeable while laity is inexperienced • Patient and family contribution is largely unnecessary	• Gradual onset over time • Multivariate causes, changing over time • Diagnosis is uncertain ad prognosis obscure • Indecisive technologies and therapies with adversities • No cure, pervasive uncertainty: management, coaching and self-care over time is needed to improve health • Professionals and laity must be reciprocally knowledgeable to improve health • Patient and family contribution critical

Table 8.4 Impact of Social Networks

Chronic disease management	85%
Promotion of healthy behaviors	78%
Emotional support	41%
Preventive care	34%
Post acute recovery	24%
Palliative care/end-of-life care	20%
Acute disease management	5%
Social networks not useful in healthcare delivery	1%

The publication confronted the existing chemical/mechanical model of the patient by explicitly by asking about the efficacy of patients' social networks, yet it does not include patients or their relatives among those surveyed. This, of course, leaves essential parts of the model intact.

Chapter 9

Genetics and the Return of Individualized Medicine

Humoral medicine recognized the individual nature of each person, and modern genetics has begun to do the same. Rather than ground such individualism in unique birth times and astrological data, it bases it on each person's unique genetic structure—as a component of the mechanical body. Individualized medicine offers a new way to separate the mechanical body from the patient who inhabits it. The expectation is that genetics will identify the inherited propensities of each person to maintain his or her health or to acquire certain diseases. If expectations are fulfilled, then people may be able to avert or defer the onset of some chronic conditions by the medical manipulation of their genetic structure. Chronic conditions like heart disease, type 2 Diabetes, and many cancers have a complex etiology, which includes genetic contributors.

Charles Darwin (1809–1882)

Modern thinking about genetics properly began with Darwin's theory of evolution, which is centered on the idea of natural selection. Charles Darwin (Figure 9.1) gathered and observed many species in his voyages and struggled to understand how they came to be differentiated. He concluded that the genetic structure of a living thing occasionally can change or mutate. Mutations can affect offspring in the next generation or in later generations. Mutations can be useful, harmful, or make no difference to the life chances of the offspring. If the change is damaging, then it can make it more difficult for progeny to survive and reproduce, so the mutation dies out and becomes an evolutionary dead end. If the change is positive, then it is likely that those offspring with the mutation will do better than others and so will reproduce more. The process of culling bad mutations and spreading good mutations is called natural selection. It can take millions of years to create new species as a result of mutations.

Charles Darwin.

Figure 9.1   Charles Darwin.

An Aside on the Evolution of Human Consciousness

Most contemporary theories of consciousness recognize that consciousness is not possible without an awareness of others. In contrast to the Cartesian picture of consciousness as logically founded on self-awareness as in "I think therefore I am," the evolutionary model of consciousness declares, "I relate to others therefore I think." Far from being isolated individual minds inside mechanical bodies, our consciousness begins with an awareness of others.

We now largely accept that mutation and natural selection are the source of every species alive today including viruses, bacteria, plants and animals. The development of modern genetics at first helped us to better understand genetic information about some individual organisms. More recently, by unraveling the genome of many particular species we have gained knowledge at the molecular level.

Francis Galton (1822–1911)

Darwin's ideas were quickly applied to human society. Herbert Spencer, the founder of Social Darwinism, coined the famous phrase "survivor of the fittest" in reference not only to animals and plants, but also to different nationalities and races. Francis Galton, Darwin's cousin, is credited with starting the eugenics movement. His book, *Inquiries into Human Faculty and Its Development* published in 1883, contained a plan for improving the human race by selectively breeding the "fittest" to make sure of their survival. He advocated "artificial selection," which would achieve results that otherwise would take much longer than "natural selection." He influenced a movement that urged the sterilization of those considered less than "fit."

The United States was the first country to implement large scale legal sterilization programs for eugenic reasons. Many intellectually challenged people were sterilized along with other vulnerable people. Carrie Buck was a 17-year-old girl from Charlottesville, Virginia. Her mother had been committed to an institution for the feeble minded, and Carrie was put in foster care. When Carrie became pregnant and had a child, she too was tried for being feeble minded (though there was no evidence of it) and then sterilized. Sterilization programs like hers were supported by the Supreme Court in 1927. Similarly, black women were sterilized, often without their knowledge, while in hospital for childbirth. About 65,000 eugenic sterilizations occurred in the United States.

The United States was hardly alone. There were eugenics movements in many countries throughout the world that resulted in forced sterilization of vulnerable populations. In Canada, for example, compulsory sterilizations stopped only in the 1970s. And just like in the US, those targeted were often vulnerable for reasons of racism or social exclusion.

Wilhelm Beiglböck (1905–1963), Karl Brandt (1904–1948), and Josef Mengele (1911–1979)

Eugenics was embraced in Nazi Germany. Nazi doctors and medical scientists sterilized more than 600,000 German citizens for eugenic reasons. Here they included not only the mentally unfit, but also homosexuals, Jews, Romany, and others. During the World War II, a good part of the justification for the mass extermination of Jews was that it was a eugenic procedure to purify the "fittest" Aryan race.

In the concentration camps, Josef Mengele experimented on almost 1,500 sets of identical twins in order to see what features could be manipulated in genetically identical subjects. He injected them with various diseases, attempted to change their eye color, and sewed them together to see if he could create Siamese twins.

Medical experimentation on human subjects tortured and killed thousands of concentration camp prisoners, who were considered to be dispensable experimental material. People were immersed in cold water to see how long it took to die of hypothermia; others were infected with tuberculosis to study immunity from the disease; biological weapons were tested on human subjects; limbs were transplanted from one person to another.

The Max Planck Institute for Brain Research is considered to be one of the founding research centers for neuroscience. The large number of brain specimens it collected during the war from patients, who were "euthanized" because they were mentally handicapped, Jewish, homosexual, or physically disabled, were retained after the war and finally buried in 1990.

The Doctor Trials at Nuremberg resulted in punishment for some of these activities and a code of ethics was formally accepted. Karl Brandt, who had been Hitler's doctor, authorized forced euthanasia during the war. He was tried in Nuremberg and executed in 1948. Wilhelm Beiglböck who performed experiments on the ingestion of sea water, during which many subjects died excruciatingly painful deaths, was jailed for ten years. The notorious Josef Mengele performed many twin experiments, which are still used to examine the similarities and differences between people with identical genetic structures. He eluded capture and drowned while swimming off the coast of Brazil.

Here are the ten points of the Nuremberg Code that introduced a basis of ethical conduct with experimental subjects.

1. The voluntary, well-informed, understanding consent of the human subject in a full legal capacity is required.
2. The experiment should aim at positive results for society that cannot be procured in some other way.

3. It should be based on previous knowledge (like, an expectation derived from animal experiments) that justifies the experiment.
4. The experiment should be set up in a way that avoids unnecessary physical and mental suffering and injuries.
5. It should not be conducted when there is any reason to believe that it implies a risk of death or disabling injury.
6. The risks of the experiment should be in proportion to (that is, not exceed) the expected humanitarian benefits.
7. Preparations and facilities must be provided that adequately protect the subjects against the experiment's risks.
8. The staff that conduct or take part in the experiment must be fully trained and scientifically qualified.
9. The human subjects must be free to immediately quit the experiment at any point when they feel physically or mentally unable to go on.
10. Likewise, the medical staff must stop the experiment at any point when they observe that continuation would be dangerous.

Rosalind Franklin (1920–1958), Francis Crick (1916–2004), and James Watson (1928–)

James Watson and Francis Crick first published the structure of DNA in 1953. Their work was based on the X-Ray images created by Rosalind Franklin and later Maurice Wilkins. This fundamental research has had enormous impact on biology and medicine.

Herbert Boyer (1936–) and Stanley Cohen (1935–)

For example, it led to the introduction of genetic engineering in 1973. Herbert Boyer and Stanley Cohen first genetically engineered cells by cutting out a gene from one organism and pasting into another. Their efforts produced chemicals like the human growth hormone, synthetic insulin, factor VIII for hemophilia, and others. Herbert Boyer was a founder of Genentech a major biotechnology company engaged in bio engineering in 1976.

This new technology opened countless avenues of research possibilities including the development of genetically engineered foods. The great success of this effort has meant that between 60% and 70% of food in North America is grown from genetically modified seed. The controversy surrounding these foods includes questions about their long-term safety, and the right of consumers to know if their food has been genetically engineered. At the moment, these foods are not labelled as genetically modified in some countries, such as the United Stated and Canada. Only foods that are labelled as organic are certified as not genetically engineered.

Charles DeLisi (1941–), Pete Domenici (1932–), and Craig Venter (1946–)

The project of decoding the human genome was envisaged once the structure of DNA had been established in 1953. The project was proposed in 1984 and began in earnest in 1990. It brought together large government resources through the efforts of Pete Domenici, then senator from New Mexico, academic scientists like Charles DeLisi the Metcalfe Professor of Science and Engineering at Boston University, and private sector entrepreneurs like Craig Venter the founder of Celera Genomics and the J. Craig Venter Institute. To all intents and purposes, success was declared in 2003. The results and the techniques used to achieve them suggested that future research will be quicker and even more fruitful.

Angelina Jolie (1975–)

Perhaps the most famous person to benefit from the increased understanding of the human genome is the film actress Angelina Jolie. She learned about a defective gene that dramatically increased her risk of breast cancer and ovarian cancer and underwent a series of operations to remove those organs. She made her situation public in a New York Times op-ed with the expressed hope of alerting and helping other women better use this genetic information.

Emmanuelle Charpentier (1968–) and Jennifer Doudna (1964–)

Jennifer Doudna and Emmanuelle Charpentier are two scientists closely associated with the discovery and use of Clustered Regularly Interspaced Short Palindromic Repeats (CRISPR), a molecule found in bacteria that allows for editing DNA code. Scientists can now target any genetic sequence, turn genes off, or replace them with new versions. CRISPR has helped to quickly produce genetically modified mice with specific characteristics for research purposes by editing their genes rather than by breeding them over multiple generations. Scientists have so far managed to correct the genetic conditions that cause muscular dystrophy in mice.

CRISPR is already being used to develop new foods. The US Department of Agriculture has permitted a CRISPR edited white mushroom to be sold without GMO regulation since developers avoided using new genetic material by removing the gene for an enzyme from the mushroom itself to stop it from browning.

The editing of human embryos is next, although it is still controversial because edited genes can be passed on to future generations. Nonetheless CRISPR-edited embryos are already being studied in China and will be studied by scientists in Great Britain in the near future.

Discoveries in genetics have allowed us to provide a completely individual account of each person's genetic makeup and, ultimately, allowed for highly individualized diagnosis and treatment based on our unique genetic character. The rekindled interest in "personalized medicine" is to some extent being driven by the promise of the development we have described in genetics. For a fee we can find out a great deal about our genetic makeup, from the propensity for certain diseases to tolerances for some medications.

Genetic researchers have emphasized that our health is not a function only of our genetic makeup. Our personal life goals, the environmental context, our individual behaviors, and a very large number of social/relational variables can make a much greater contribution to the health of most us than our individual DNA. There are a small number of genetically determined conditions that affect a relatively small part of the population. Despite the wide agreement among geneticists that genetics plays a very limited role in most chronic diseases, the public media focuses on the somewhat mechanical genetic correlations with the disease. While this is immensely valuable, it only explains a small fraction of the causes of the most common chronic diseases including heart disease, respiratory diseases, diabetes, and cancers.

Chapter 10

The Great Mortality Shift

In 1800, the average longevity at birth across the world was
between 25 and 40 years as it had been from prehistoric
times. Since then the increase in world life expectancy at birth
has continued unabated and seems likely to continue for at
least some years. A recent figure for worldwide longevity is
71.4 years for everyone born in 2015. This rise of more than
thirty years in average longevity has continued despite wars,
epidemics, famine, and other large-scale causes of mortality.
It is projected to continue to increase at least until late in this
century.

There is some dispute about when the Great Mortality
Shift began. For some time, it was thought that this increase
in longevity at birth began in the middle of the nineteenth
century when public health efforts to clean the environment
began, but there is a growing agreement that it started earlier.
Because of uncertainty about birth and death records before
the nineteenth century there is no widespread agreement
about an exact start time.

Edwin Chadwick (1800–1890)

In many histories of medicine, the increase in longevity is claimed to have begun after the passage of the first Public Health Act of 1848 in England and is attributed to Edwin Chadwick, the father of public health. Chadwick, the earliest and most vigorous proponent of sanitation in the nineteenth century, is considered in medical histories to be the main champion of the Act. His friendship with Jeremy Bentham and John Stuart Mill encouraged him to become an active social reformer. Chadwick first joined and then became Secretary of the Commission to revise the Poor Laws in England (1834). Not satisfied with the resulting Act, he argued for improved sanitation for all. As a statistician, he gathered data to make his arguments and, in 1842, he self-published the *Report on the Sanitary Condition of the Labouring Population*, which showed that the chance to survive to adulthood followed environmental conditions. He found that highest mortality rate of infants and young children occurred in cities where sanitation was the poorest and the lowest rate was in rural areas with more clean water and less contaminated sewage. Longevity at birth was closely related to the sanitary environment.

Deep in his report Chadwick suggested that people were living longer; that is, a mortality shift had already started. He attributed this to an increase in both "happiness and prosperity," but primarily to a reduced number of (very dangerous) pregnancies and a reduction in infant mortality. The following passage was largely ignored.

> The progression of the population and the increased duration of life had been attended by a progression in happiness: as prosperity advanced marriages became fewer and later; the proportion of births was reduced, but greater numbers of the infants born were preserved; and the proportion of the population

in manhood became greater. In the early and barbarous periods, the excessive mortality was accomplished by a prodigious fecundity. In the ten last years of the seventeenth century, a marriage still produced five children and more; the probable duration of life attained was not 20 years, and Geneva had scarcely 17,000 inhabitants. Towards the end of the eighteenth century there were scarcely three children to a marriage, and the probabilities of life exceeded 32 years. At the present time a marriage only produces 2 ¾ children; the probability of life is 45 years, and Geneva, which exceeds 27,000 in population, has arrived at a high degree of civilization and of *prosperité materielle.*

Chadwick was not a doctor. He was strongly influenced by the social/relational views of Bentham and Mill. He did not base his arguments for improved sanitation on the germ theory. As a sanitarian, he accepted the miasma theory of illness from Galen's time that filth, dirty water, and polluted air were the cause of disease. This put him in conflict with much of the mechanical medical establishment of that era, who were opposed to the increasingly discredited miasma theory but had not yet unanimously accepted the germ theory. Prominent scientists of the day, like Rudolph Virchow, the father of modern pathology and enemy of Ignaz Semmelweis, were skeptical of the germ theory, dismissed the miasma theory, and instead argued that weather and individual vulnerabilities caused the epidemics that killed large numbers of people, especially infants.

Despite Chadwick's continuing fights with the medical establishment, his desire for more complete and accurate statistical data led him to argue for making a doctor's signature necessary on all death certificates to improve record keeping. Ironically this requirement became a major step in the modern professionalization of doctors in England because it formalized who counted as a doctor. In some medical histories, Chadwick is acclaimed as a critical figure in the struggle to make academic doctors true professionals with control over their discipline.

Chadwick worked for years towards the passage of the Public Health Act of 1848. (This is what most likely led some historians to identify the mid-nineteenth century as the start of the mortality shift and to appropriate Chadwick as the father of Public Health.) The Act created local health boards to supervise the cleanliness of water, to maintain the sewage capacity of towns, and to assure that housing was not overcrowded. However, because of strong opposition from vested interests, the first Public Health Act was only a small step towards improved public health. There remained many privately owned unregulated water supply companies whose sources were frequently contaminated. Sewage systems in cities, like London were incomplete, primitive, and largely unregulated. It is not clear how increased longevity at birth could be ascribed to Chadwick's first public health Bill. Chadwick himself was not satisfied with the bill and continued to fight for stronger measures for the rest of his life.

John Snow (1813–1858)

Poor sewage systems and impure water supply lasted until the late nineteenth century. The cholera epidemic of 1854 is well known because of the exceedingly careful and brilliant epidemiological work of John Snow, who isolated its source to a water pump on Broad Street in Soho, London. Because it took a long time to convince officials to remove the pump handle, the epidemic gradually waned. As a result, it was not entirely clear that his intervention ended the epidemic, though he had clearly pinpointed its origin.

Joseph Bazalgette (1818–1891)

Less well known today is the Great Stink in London of 1858. During the summer of that year, the inadequate sewer system, coupled with excessively hot weather, resulted in untreated human waste being deposited on the shores of the Thames, sometimes to a depth of six feet. The defining moment came when Queen Victoria and Prince Albert attempted to take a cruise on the river but gave up because of the terrible smell. The Press declared there was no further need for gentility— they had to report that the river did indeed stink! A decision to build a modern sewer system followed. It was completed in 1875 under the supervision of Joseph Bazalgette. The underlying rationale for this effort was still the Galenic miasma theory of illness.

John Simon (1816–1876)

In 1875, a second, more stringent Public Health Bill passed as a result of the efforts of many reformers led by John Simon. The sanitation system was further strengthened: all new housing had to have running water and an internal drainage system connected to a public sewer system. This second Public Health Bill was a major contributor to sanitary conditions in London, to public health and, of course, to longevity.

Access to healthcare became another critical objective of the growing public health movement that urged an increased sense of responsibility for the health of the population. The burgeoning wealth of cities and towns led to the creation of more accessible health services for the poor and the working class. Even before modern hospitals were built there were dispensaries with free prescription drugs and publicly funded home care services for the poor. Later in the century,

Germany, under Bismarck, initiated health insurance with partial contributions from workers.

At the time of the Boer War, the health condition of army recruits in Great Britain was very poor. Many of their health issues could be resolved by medical interventions. Reformers began the long argument for state sponsored healthcare; almost 50 years later the NHS was established. Bentham, Mill, Chadwick, and later Simon had argued in favor of more state accountability for the health of its citizens. Like most other reforms, this one took a long time to implement.

The National Insurance Act (NIA) of 1911 provided health insurance for primary care, a first step towards universal health care benefit in the UK. The NIA provided for the services of primary care doctors as well as income to cover part of the wage loss of workers. It was one of many reforms in health, housing, education and electoral reform sponsored by the Liberal government of the day.

Aneurin Bevan (1897–1960)

When the mortality shift was first noticed after World War II it was quickly ascribed to the acceptance of the mechanical model of the body. Medical science using that model had demonstrated the germ theory and developed numerous vaccines for infectious diseases. Similarly, the introduction of anesthesia and antiseptic surgical procedures, the modern hospital, and later the discovery of antibiotics, showed that we could be optimistic about conquering most diseases. Little wonder that increased longevity was ascribed to medical progress.

Britain, like many European countries, established a universal healthcare system soon after World War II. The (National Health Service) NHS had been in the planning stage since the Dawson Report was commissioned. Its establishment was closely preceded by the wartime Beveridge Report. The great successes of medical science and the belief that the NHS would improve the health of the population, and, in so doing, reduce demand for healthcare were major arguments for it. It was finally launched in 1948 by Aneurin Bevan who set three principles:

- That it met the needs of everyone
- That it be free at the point of delivery
- That it be based on clinical need, not ability to pay

It also had three areas of responsibility:

Hospital Care included all care in hospitals including acute care and emergency services and was under the direction of 14 Regions.

Primary Care included services of GPs, Dentists, Pharmacists and Opticians as independent contractors to the NHS. Their contracts were monitored by executive Councils.

Community Care included maternity and child welfare clinics, health visitors, midwives, health education, vaccination and immunization and ambulance services together with environmental health services. These services had been the responsibility of local authorities since the time of Chadwick.

The NHS was a major addition to the welfare state in the UK. It became and remains a well-loved government service and no government, however conservative, dares threaten its existence. Unexpectedly, the demand for healthcare services continued to increase. For our purposes it is important to note that access to even mechanical health services is not itself a chemical/mechanical advance, but rather a social change—one which provides services to the population.

The NHS was only one aspect of the optimistic mid-twentieth century view of the scientific future, but another was that an even greater control over the physical environment would allow humans to benefit from the fruits of scientific progress. Huge engineering projects were launched to tame unruly shorelines. Research was funded to help control other aspects of the environment including the weather. The promise was the fulfilment of Francis Bacon's vision: that our ability to control nature would continue to improve our lives.

Rachel Carson (1907–1964)

However, the promise of increased environmental control soon began to erode (like the beaches). The consequences of damming rivers, building canals, and draining swamps, accompanied by the widespread use of dichlorodiphenyltri-chloroethane (DDT) and other chemicals, raised concerns about the effect on local species and diminishing biodiversity. We began to realize that the Baconian promise that science would give us control over nature was misguided (Figure 10.1).

Figure 10.1   Rachel Carson.

In 1962, Rachel Carson published *Silent Spring,* a warning about the damaging effects of DDT on the natural environment. Its title is taken from one chapter on the effect of such insecticides on birds. Although it was later shown that many of Carson's claims were overstated, the book sparked a shift in public attitude and led to a growing realization that humans are part of nature, not its highest form, and that we must learn to respect our environment. Ecological views of the future encouraged green spaces, "natural" foods, solar and wind power, and discouraged the enormous energy consumption of personal jet planes, and gigantic mechanized cityscapes. The green movement had started.

Thomas McKeown (1912–1988)

At the same time Thomas McKeown was studying the medical and health landscape of the mortality shift. He argued that increased longevity was not due primarily to medical innovation. He introduced the term "determinants of health" to stand for various sources of increased longevity. He argued that the major determinants of improvement in health in England and Wales primarily were a result of the social and physical environment of a person: (1) the increase in food supplies, a nutritional change which improved people's resistance to infectious diseases and, (2) echoing Chadwick, limitations of family size—a behavioral change which reduced infant and maternal mortality, and (3) finally, and least important, to specific preventive and therapeutic medical measures. Unlike Rachel Carson's book, McKeown's early papers on the subject were not well received.

Today, there is still no agreement about the precise causes of the mortality shift. Although there have been many arguments against McKeown's specific explanations, none have denied his major claim that modern medicine is only one factor in increased longevity. His views became much more influential after they were integrated into a Canadian document that attained an international reception.

Hubert Laframboise (1924–1991) and Marc Lalonde (1929–)

That we no longer think of health as a product only of medical science but as a consequence of other determinants, is in no small measure due to the Lalonde Report, *Towards a New Perspective on the Health of Canadians*. Its publication in 1974 initiated a pronounced shift in thinking about health and social policy. Soon after the report was issued international movements began to argue for health promotion in addition to medical care.

The Lalonde Report is named for the then Minister of Health and Welfare, Marc Lalonde, but it was actually written under the leadership of Hubert (Bert) Laframboise, an Assistant Deputy Minister in the Federal Department of Health and Welfare where he created a "free-wheeling think tank" with which to inform government policy discussions.

The ideas developed by McKeown about health and health policy in his early papers deeply influenced their approach. The report accepts McKeown's central idea that one had to go beyond standard medical services to improve the health of the population.

The Lalonde Report identifies four major determinants of health and speaks of them as constituting a "Health Field." The following table describes the four quadrants of the health field (Table 10.1).

(In more modern terms, *Environment* includes not only the physical environment but also the social determinants of health, *Lifestyle*, individual control over health, *Human Biology*, the nature of the chemical/mechanical body, *Healthcare Organization*, the Medical healthcare system.)

Table 10.1 The Health Field Concept

Environment	Lifestyle
All matters related to health external to the human body and over which the individual has little or no control. Includes the physical and social environment.	The aggregation of personal decisions, over which the individual has control. Self-imposed risks created by unhealthy lifestyle choices can be said to contribute to, or cause, illness, or death.
Human Biology	**Healthcare Organization**
All aspects of health, physical and mental, developed within the human body as a result of organic make-up.	The quantity, quality, arrangement, nature, and relationships of people and resources in the provision of healthcare.

A New Perspective on the Health of Canadians remains one of the most significant government documents produced in Canada. The Lalonde Report spawned a steadily growing international movement for health promotion. By 1977, 140,000 copies had been distributed, and it was hailed as a world-class document. It became an integral part of health promotion policy in many countries, including the United States. It also marked a dramatic shift in increasing individuals' responsibility for their own health. By 1984, it was heralded as "one of the great achievements of the modern public health movement." In 1986, it was made the basis for the Ottawa Charter for Health Promotion, which remains a key element of health promotion internationally, especially in developing countries. Foreign visitors to Ottawa from small developing countries, who have devoted their lives to improving the health at home, often ask to see the Ottawa Charter, for which there is, unfortunately, no monument.

Following are some examples of major changes in lifestyle that have occurred since the publication of the report.

Smoking: At the time of the Lalonde Report more than 35% of adults smoked in North America. The percentage is now less than 20%. Policies and citizen led campaigns to reduce smoking have had a strong impact on smoking cessation. According to *Cancer: The Emperor of All Diseases* by S. Mukerjee smoking reduction campaigns have had a far greater impact on cancer reduction than all the billions of dollars spent on cancer research.

Seatbelts: The use of seatbelts was voluntary at the time of the Lalonde Report which recommended that it be made mandatory. Seatbelt legislation resulted in a significantly lower mortality rate in road accidents.

Physical exercise: At the time of the Lalonde Report moderate exercise meant going to the gym three times a month. Policies and programs encouraged fitness training, and increased physical activity, such as walking 10,000 steps a day, and going to the gym at least three times a week. The fitness industry has produced portable electronic devices to measure and record physical activity on an ongoing basis.

Nutrition: In 1974 most North Americans ate red meat and few green vegetables. Food Guides had been relatively inactive since WWII and did not provide direction on appropriate fats, sugars and caloric intake. New Food Guides appeared soon after the Lalonde Report which recommended less red meat and more fruits and green vegetables. Most North Americans have significantly changed their eating habits since.

Organic growers emerged in the 1970s soon after the Lalonde Report was published. At that time, organic foods were sold in the back part of very few health food stores. Regulated organic food is now sold in every major supermarket in North America. Chains of supermarkets now specialize in organic and other healthy food because there is a much wider concern about nutrition and food safety. The lack of labeling of genetically engineered agricultural produce in North America has become a policy issue.

Perhaps the greatest impact of the Lalonde Report was the dramatic increase of people taking responsibility for their own health. Today information technology has given us smart phones, which allow us to monitor many of the resources that contribute to our health. More than 100,000 smartphone apps are devoted to health. There is little doubt now that this technology will transform our interactions with clinicians. We are already able to use computers to do many things: we can access our medical test results and know what they mean; we can learn far more about our health conditions; we can record our health history and articulate our health goals; we can communicate with others who suffer from the conditions that affect us; and some of us can even make appointments with our doctors.

Soon we will be able to use computer-based programs to monitor the state of our health and diagnose a wide variety of conditions. There are already otoscope attachments for our phones that allow us to photograph our children's inner ears and send the photo to the doctor for diagnosis without the need for a live visit. These programs will soon be able to compare the photos we take with a database and diagnose infections with no need for the doctor. There are similar smartphone attachments that will perform electrocardiograms and compare them with previous tests within a database to see what changes have occurred in order to diagnose emerging issues. A large number of new apps appear daily with surprisingly innovative uses. Health information about individuals can already be sent through the internet with full security using Blockchain technology. Patients will soon gain control of the content and have more complete access to their medical information.

The increase in patients' capacity to participate actively in their health is already forcing a change in the relationship between patients and doctors. Active patients bring more information, more questions and many specific suggestions to their meetings with their doctors. Because these active patients share an acceptance of the chemical/mechanical model of the body, most doctors welcome their participation.

Like other healthcare innovations, the increase in patient participation in their own healthcare promised a healthier society and a drop in the use of healthcare services. However, the opposite has occurred. There has been a constant increase in the cost of healthcare and in the number of users of its services. For example, more exercise has resulted in more knee and hip replacements. Kenneth Arrow, the father of health economics, claimed that healthcare unlike most other parts of the economy is supply rather than demand driven: the more medical services that are offered, the greater the demand will be for them. Every major innovation in healthcare over the last hundred years has increased the supply of care and promised that a healthier population will result with a lower demand on healthcare services. In every case the opposite has been true. More healthcare services have always increased the demand. Kenneth Arrow appears to have been correct.

Medicine today has an enormous capacity to diagnose and treat the chemical/mechanical body. It can identify chemical imbalances, detect malfunctioning organs, and use advanced technology to perform very complex surgical procedures. A growing number of drugs are specific to particular, ever rarer conditions. The new genetics will allow individualized treatment by identifying genetic propensities.

We continue to live longer. Some argue that the maximum life span of human beings is about 120 years. Everything else being equal, we could reach that maximum by the end of the twenty-first century. There are others who reply that with improvements in medical science the maximum age of humans will increase before then and will continue to increase indefinitely; there will be no limit to the extension of life expectancy at birth. By the end of this century. we will have a pretty good idea about which of these claims is correct. Recently it was predicted that there will be an increase in the average longevity of women in South Korea to a little over 90 for those born in 2030–we wonder if that estimate is too low.

Chapter 11

Humanizing Health: The Social/Relational Person

Humans are not isolated individual minds inside chemical/ mechanical bodies, but social animals whose interaction with each other define who we are as a species. Intuitively we understand the limitations of the mechanical model, which separates our bodies from us. Nor are we so separate from other people. We are born into families, and we live in communities. Our earliest ideas of a happy and healthy life are social. They come from what little we know, and some of what we fantasize about when we think of prehistoric hunter-gatherers. Much of the literature claims that they lived in small bands with strong social relationships but little formal organization. They made few distinctions between the roles of men and women, and decisions were made by consensus. These early humans are almost always said to have lived well and to have been relatively healthy. They spent no more than two hours a day gathering food and had leisure for the rest of the day; playing with their children, socializing with other tribe members, and resting. They were not affected by infectious diseases, which require a larger population in which to spread.

The women had much less pain from childbirth because stooping to forage strengthened their birthing muscles. Many descriptions of the earliest humans are positive, even idyllic, like life in the Garden of Eden. Though some of this is most likely fantasy, it can serve as a somewhat sentimental account of a desirable social/relational healthy life that disappeared with the coming of agriculture.

The intensification of populations made it impossible to continue as hunter-gatherers and stopped that kind of life from being widely available, although some aspects of it have continued in ever smaller and more remote places until today. The beginnings of agriculture coincided with the introduction of land ownership that distinguished those who owned land from those who worked on it—some as slaves. Increased density of the population also brought more disease. Germs from domestic animals evolved to affect humans so that we began to share diseases with animals. Measles came from dogs, influenzas from pigs and ducks, colds from horses, and smallpox and other viruses from cattle. There is little in the literature about who was healthy and who was not; but it would be fair to assume that there were important differences in the potential for a happy and healthy life between owners and their slaves. Early Proto-Elamite tablets tell us that the rations of agricultural slaves consisted of weak beer and porridge while honey, fresh fruits, and yogurt was part of the diet of their owners.

By the time we get to Ancient Greece, it is clear not everyone had the resources to live a good life. Aristotle accepted as given a clearly defined hierarchical society that limited the roles of women, foreigners, tradesmen and slaves, and the resources for a good and happy life were not distributed to all. One had to have the luck to be born first as a male, and then as a full citizen (an active component of the state) to have access to all the resources needed for *eudaimonia*—happiness, or a good life.

The Aristotelian concept of *eudaimonia* is in sharp contrast to medieval Christian ideas about a good life. For mediaeval thinkers, a good life was one that led to salvation. The stress was on virtuous piety in preparation for life after death, rather than happiness in this life. There was little emphasis on other resources. This shift in the idea of a good life transferred its rewards from the everyday world to a world after death where one received one's deserts for devout behavior in this world. Salvation was available to all virtuous and devout Christians. In contrast to Aristotle, the mediaeval view was that if you died of torture in order to achieve salvation, you might very well have lived an exemplary life, could certainly go to heaven, and might even be canonized.

The Great Chain of Being

It is noteworthy that the ancient social hierarchies became even more extreme in the mediaeval context. The status and authority of kings, the nobility and clerics were sanctioned by god as well as the state. The Great Chain of Being described an essentially hierarchical world. This mediaeval religious conception of the relation between this life and the world to come was not fundamentally revised during the Renaissance; however, the extremely hierarchical nature of society began to flatten and the secularization of society began to erode its religious orientation. After the Black Plague, serfs obtained more freedom and a middle class of secular merchants gained wealth and social status. More people had resources to lead better lives before death, but salvation after death remained a central goal.

The shift to thinking that everyone could have a good and a happy life before an afterlife was one indication of the beginnings of modernity evident in seventeenth century thinkers like John Locke. He went much farther, perhaps because he lived during the only time when the English executed their king and became a republic. Locke argued for the fundamental equality of all citizens. He also believed that every citizen had the right to pursue a good life and to accumulate the resources needed for it. He argued for religious toleration so that the many Christian sects, which had multiplied through the seventeenth century, could coexist, and that individual citizens could pursue a good life within their beliefs. Locke held that the state gains its power by means of a social contract with its citizens. The citizens accept the state's authority and the state has an obligation to protect and promote the well-being of its citizens: the state enables the accumulation of resources or "property" for a good life. Locke's ideas about "life, liberty and the pursuit of property" were later restated by Thomas Jefferson in the American Declaration of Independence as "life, liberty and the pursuit of happiness." For the deeply religious Locke, a successful government fulfills God's purpose for mankind—to enable people to flourish both economically and spiritually. (It should be pointed out that to our contemporary eyes the exclusion of women and slaves from citizenship during this period is a fundamental omission.)

Voltaire (1694–1778), Rousseau (1712–1778), Diderot (1713–1784), and Hume (1711–1776)

The Enlightenment and Reform

Reform was at the core of the Enlightenment. Voltaire (François-Marie Arouet), Jean-Jacques Rousseau, Denis Diderot, and David Hume were prominent eighteenth century participants in the movement. Rational deduction and experimentation were at the center of its scientific commitment, and social/relational reform was its political manifestation. Reform movements began in many countries. The American Revolution was deeply influenced by these ideas. In France they reached a culmination with the French Revolution in 1789, with the demand for "Liberty, equality, fraternity!"

James Edward Oglethorpe (1696–1785)

The abolition of slavery is an excellent example of an enlightenment social reform just before the beginning of the nineteenth century. The lives of slaves were always significantly
shorter than those of their masters: they lived under worse
conditions, were underfed, badly housed, and many were
literally worked to death, especially in the colonies. Their offspring often did not survive. Chances of a good and happy life
were negligible.

The Enlightenment was a major influence on the
abolitionist movement. James Oglethorpe was a member of
parliament in 1728. He first argued for a reform of the terrible
conditions experienced by sailors in the British Royal Navy.
(Vast numbers were forcibly recruited, and then killed by
scurvy rather than military action.) He chaired a committee
on prison reform which documented the abuses suffered by
inmates in debtors' prisons. He led the movement to resettle
debtors and other prisoners in the new colony of Georgia in
America. Oglethorpe went there as governor to establish a
community with a small-scale economy made up of family
farms distributed by land grants. There was to be no slavery
at all, and indentured servants were to receive their own land
grants after completing their debt of service. Needless to say,
it did not work out quite that way in Georgia and the other
southern states. However, Oglethorpe's ideas set the stage for
the abolition of slavery in England and the British Empire.

The increase of life expectancy at birth in the United
Kingdom began not in 1850, but in the late eighteenth and
early nineteenth century. In the late eighteenth century slavery was abolished not only in Britain but also in Portugal
and Russia. There were effective movements to put an end
to the slave trade around the world. By the early nineteenth
century, with some notable exceptions, slavery was abolished in most European countries, in many of their colonies,
and throughout South America. There is some evidence that

the abolition of slavery contributed to the mortality shift by improving the health and wellbeing of former slaves and especially their children.

Jeremy Bentham (1748–1832) and John Stuart Mill (1806–1873)

Abolition of slavery and other social relational reforms were advocated by Jeremy Bentham and John Stuart Mill, the originators of Utilitarianism. They argued that it was the role of the state to achieve "the greatest happiness for the greatest number" of people. Bentham's notion of happiness can be compared with Aristotle's *eudaimonia.* Both had ideas of happiness linked to conceptions of living a good life, to well-being and to "human flourishing." Bentham gave equal value to straightforward individualism and social pleasure. While for Aristotle a good life was comprised of active participation and virtuous living, and, ultimately, was to be philosophically contemplated in retrospect. Both Bentham and Aristotle shared the view that resources are needed to enable people to achieve happiness and well-being. A great difference between them is that Aristotle accepted the gradations of society as a natural unchangeable phenomenon and never considered class reform. In contrast to Bentham, Aristotle believed in the natural inferiority of women and accepted the institution of slavery along with great limitations on who could participate in the political activity of the state. Bentham argued that everyone should be free and able to participate politically.

At the end of the eighteenth and beginning of the nineteenth century, Bentham argued for a broad range of social and relational reforms, including equal status for women, parliamentary reform, universal suffrage, an end to slavery, the right to divorce, and the decriminalization of homosexuality. He was committed to changing the nature of criminal punishment, including the abolition of the death penalty, the dramatic redesign of prisons, and the abolition of physical punishment of children and adults. He introduced new ideas about education and the relation between teachers and student and was active in founding University College London—the first secular university in England.

The influence of Bentham, Mill, and other reformers extended through the nineteenth century and into the twentieth century with the development of policies intended to provide resources to enable everyone to pursue good and happy lives. Only a small part of these reforms can be considered as part of public health or based on the mechanical model. The distribution of such Aristotelian goods as education, leisure, shelter, and political participation eventually became widespread through compulsory publicly-funded education, maximum working hours, minimum wage, the right to strike, universal suffrage, graduated income tax, and other similar reforms. Such reforms were meant to reduce inequality and provide social/relational resources for living well.

The Lalonde Report did not consider that the impact of publicly funded health promotion would be affected by social inequality. Today, 40 years after the Lalonde Report was issued, the important gains described in the previous chapter are still not equally distributed. Smoking cessation has been very successful in upper income communities. Although overall smoking has dropped to less than 20% of the population overall, there is a disparity in smoking cessation that follows socio-economic status (SES). In fact, people with lower SES continue to smoke at almost the same levels as the general population did in 1974. As for exercise, Statistics Canada reported that even though Canadians with higher SES have less leisure time than others, they spend more absolute time on exercise and fitness activities. Similar disparities in physical activity occur in most other developed countries. Finally, despite overall gains in healthy eating and the greater availability of healthy foods, nutritional impact on health also follows class lines. Obesity has become the mark of poverty not only in wealthy countries, like Canada, but in much of the developing world. The diet of the poor is richer in processed carbohydrates and poorer in fresh fruits and vegetables. The percentage of adults who eat five or more portions of fresh fruit and vegetables a day follows socio-economic status: the better-off eat more fruits and vegetables, the poorer eat fewer. Organic foods and specially prepared health foods remain much more easily available to the well-off.

Richard Wilkinson (1943–)

Several years after the Lalonde Report was published, Richard Wilkinson, then a research student at the University of Nottingham in England, wrote a public letter to David Ennals, the Secretary of State for Social Services at the time, and prodded the Labor government to establish a task force to investigate growing health inequalities. The result was the Black Report issued in 1980 some months after Margaret Thatcher and the Conservative Party had come into power. The Black Report confirmed Wilkinson's initial findings—although longevity and overall health had increased since the creation of the NHS, there were growing health inequalities. The Thatcher government released only 250 mimeographed copies of the report to the press. (Two of them found their way to the King's Fund where I had a chance to read the original report.) It was republished as a Penguin paperback and spurred national concern about inequalities in health. The report showed that although longevity for all had increased since the establishment of the National Health Service, inequalities in longevity had also increased. Those who were at the top of the socio-economic scale were living significantly longer than those at the bottom.

Michael Marmot (1945–)

The Whitehall Study, led by Michael Marmot, was completed in 1977. It compared the mortality of the different grades of British civil servants. The level of mortality due to heart disease was inversely correlated with a person's grade; the higher the level, the longer one would live. There was also a correlation of risk factors amongst the civil service grades including obesity, high blood pressure, smoking, less leisure time, less physical activity, more underlying illness, and shorter height. After controlling for these chemical/mechanical factors, the lowest grade still had a higher risk of dying of a heart attack than the highest grade. This meant that social/relational interactions rather than chemical/mechanical factors might be significant contributors to longevity, and hence to overall health of people. The argument displayed serious deficiencies of the mechanical model of health.

In the work of Marmot, Wilkinson, and others, the four quadrants described in the Lalonde Report evolved to become a much larger number of "social determinants of health," which included social, developmental, economic, political, and cultural factors. Similar studies in the UK and elsewhere confirmed that health inequalities followed class lines internationally.

The variables that account for health disparities are not only chemical or mechanical and cannot be resolved only by chemical or mechanical interventions: medicines, surgical procedures, diets and exercise regimens would not solve the problem. The conclusion of the inequalities in health research is clear and unequivocal. Medicine and genetic factors are not the only or even the most critical contributors to health. This echoes the claims made by Thomas McKeown, but its conclusions are more far-reaching. They force us to rethink the mechanical model of the patient that has been the philosophical basis of medical research since Robert Boyle in the seventeenth century.

Inequalities in health have not been reduced by publicly funded healthcare, or by public health measures and health promotion. The emerging model of human health recognizes that a major contributor to health is general well-being—what we have called "living a good life." This requires the kind of resources described by Aristotle and Bentham, rather than more healthcare on the mechanical model. A better distribution of the social resources needed for a good life becomes a critical factor in measuring and improving health.

These studies explain why the greatest users of mechanical healthcare systems are people with the lowest socio-economic status. They have the fewest resources for living well. They tend to be older, former daily smokers, physically inactive, obese, with multiple chronic conditions and poor self-rated health status. In Ontario, Canada, expenditure on 1/3 of the healthcare budget is spent on the top 1% of healthcare users. In the United States, this same top 1% of users accounts for 21% of healthcare costs.

These high users of healthcare do not have the resources to care for themselves when they are ill. A good example of situations that recur was described a long time ago in Ted Kennedy's 1972 book *In Critical Condition: The Crisis in America's Health Care.*

> Mr. Tillery, who lived alone, had a complete laryngectomy at the age of fifty-six. He was left unable to speak. Just over two weeks after the operation, Mr. Tillery was sent home from the hospital. He was given a list of specific equipment necessary for his care; namely, a humidifier and a tracheal suction. He was also given a list of agencies where he could find the equipment. Mr. Tillery was only able to acquire a humidifier, and not a very effective one at that. The suction, he was told, would have to be rented at a cost of 20 dollars a month.

Not two days later, Mr. Tillery unable to breathe, woke a neighbor and was sent to the emergency room. Financially, Mr. Tillery did not have much savings, enough to last him 2 or 3 months, and the $20 necessary to rent the equipment was too much for his stretched budget, which already included doctor bills.

The mechanical model of the body remains a powerful force in healthcare. Medical knowledge is growing with more subspecialties identifying an increasing number of medical conditions. There is every indication that this aspect of healthcare will continue to expand. As we become an older society, more and more people are diagnosed with chronic disease. And as new medications are found, the threshold for diagnosing such conditions has been lowered. For example, in the United States over 29 million people (of whom 25% are undiagnosed) are said to have type 2 Diabetes. Many are obese members of lower socio-economic groups. Medications will be prescribed for most of them rather than non-pharmacological alternatives of diet and physical activity because they do not have the ability or the resources to make use of these alternatives.

There have been polemics about the excessive influence of mechanical medical interests. Ivan Illich introduced his book, *Medical Nemesis*, by saying, "The medical establishment has become a major threat to health." He argued that the professionalization of physicians made them less responsible for the health of patients than for the retention of their status. A major factor in his argument is the continuing predominance of the mechanical model of the patient. John McKnight in his polemic article, "Demedicalization and Possibilities for Health," declared that, "There has never been a 'health consumer.' Nonetheless this mythical being has been medically engineered as the necessary commodity to meet the needs of the medical sector of our economic system." He concludes that it would be more appropriate to argue for a reduction in the inequality of social/relational resources for a good life from a platform outside the health field. This is because the mechanical model of the patient medicalizes health and limits proactive social/relational efforts to prevent disease.

Amartya Sen (1933–)

Amartya Sen is an Indian economist and winner of the Nobel Prize for his work on developmental economics. He introduced the very useful distinction between capacity and capability that is in some ways similar to Aristotle's discussion of goods and virtues. Sen points out that large numbers of people have the intellectual capacity to be politically engaged, but do not gain the capability to participate meaningfully in the political life of their country because they lack resources such as education, money, or even public transit. Sen's conclusion is that a truly democratic state has the responsibility to provide the resources needed to develop people's capacities into capabilities. He argues for the universal development of capability in politics so that all citizens could have a voice in government and clearly understand how it operates; in the economics of a country so that all people could benefit from its wealth; in the broadening of developmental opportunities to go to school and learn to engage in their communities. In a word, Sen argues for an equalization of the many social/relational resources for the well-being of all members of a society. Interestingly, he also argues for various aspects of security and safety, which he calls "negative liberties," such as freedom from coercion, assault, enslavement. Like Locke, he values the ability to retain the products one has created solely from one's own labor.

When we apply Sen's arguments to healthcare they suggest that most people have a native capacity to lead a healthy life. It is up to society to provide adequate resources to allow them to develop the capability to lead such life. At times, as in Mr. Tillery's case, it is merely money. In the case of the British Civil service, it appears to be a reduction in its extremely hierarchical nature. In yet others, it is the increased possibility of developmental social/relational interactions. The mechanical model must be supplemented with the recognition that health is a function of the social and relational interactions of a person. This may be a good beginning for the articulation of a social/relational model of the patient.

Thomas Piketty (1971–)

Thomas Piketty is a French economist who studies wealth inequalities. In his book, *Capital in the Twenty-First Century* he argues that, except for a short time in the twentieth century, there has been a continuous accumulation of capital by a small, very wealthy class over the last 200 years, because the return on capital constantly exceeds the rate of growth of real income and wages. He recognizes that differences along class lines have an enormous effect on one's way of living and proposes an international, annual progressive tax on capital. Without such a tax, the disparity between the very wealthy and everyone else will only increase. Although he is interested in the social consequences of inequality in wealth, and discusses them at length, nowhere does he mention any research into inequalities in health in his book. However, the health consequences are obvious and critical.

Finding a More Human Model of Health

When health is defined as "the level of functional and metabolic efficiency of a living organism," mechanical patients are treated as isolated individuals whose health depends on their genetic makeup, their ability to process food and medications, and on the fitness of their mechanical parts. Illnesses result from poisons they ingest, or the malfunction of their mechanical parts. The model largely excludes consideration of interactions between persons and their social environment. A broader social/relational model of the person is necessary.

The lack of social/relational variables in the chemical mechanical model is most obvious in the contents of current medical records, which include almost exclusively the chemical and mechanical assessment of patients. Even in the most advanced electronic systems, there is almost no information about their socio-economic circumstances, their personal relationships, or even their overall well-being. We now know that this information can provide relevant facts about the etiology of a patient's condition as well as indicators of future health status.

At a public level, almost all media discussions of health are restricted to mechanical advice about exercise, or chemical advice about diet. Once one becomes aware of the other contributors to health, this narrow range becomes very noticeable and somewhat shocking because it demonstrates how much we have all internalized the chemical/mechanical model of health. We treat ourselves and others as mechanical patients.

Brain researchers have long recognized the importance of social and relational factors in brain development. Instead of healthy brain development being dependent only on chemical/mechanical factors, it is accepted that it is physiologically dependent on appropriate experiences. This results in a socio/relational account of physiological development.

> The general consensus now is that the growth of specific brain structures takes place during critical periods in infancy, that brain development relies on stimulation and experiences and that it is shaped by a person's social environment. Brain development is driven by environmental influences, and this implies that a lack of relevant experiences may have lasting influence on brain development … just as food is necessary for the body to grow, stimulation is necessary to provide the brain with the raw materials needed for perceptual, cognitive and sensorimotor processes to mature.

Levels of health and wellbeing are now being measured using ideas heavily influenced by researchers like Amartya Sen. The table below is an adaptation of the efforts of several different groups. They can be easily correlated with predictors of health status and can contribute to a richer social/relational model of health (Table 11.1).

Table 11.1 Some Dimensions of Living Well

Economic	Developmental	Relational	Political	Health	Cultural
Decent Living Standards	*Access to Education*	*Having Friends and Loving Relationships*	*Participating in Public Life*	*Access to Healthcare*	*Leisure and Cultural Activities*
Adequate and safe housing	Literacy	Having a stable family with a critical number of close family and friends	Universal suffrage and exercise of meaningful vote	Medical and nursing services and medications	All forms of human expression
Living wage, meaningful work, and job security	Skill development	Belonging to a community and participating in organized activities	Ability to participate in democratic decisions beyond voting	Acceptable health status	The Arts
Access to nutritious food and clean water	Ability to function in differing social and work contexts	Trusting others	Free speech and free press and transparency of the political process	Ability to identify and take responsibility for health goals	Recreational activities
Ability to manage and use time for work and leisure	Develop capability to engage in democratic institutions	Helping people in distress	Global concerns	Self-care and close partnership with physicians and other healthcare providers	Entertainment

The National Child Development Study, initially directed by Neville Butler, considered the lives of more than 17,000 people born in Britain during the week beginning on March 3, 1958. It looked at the cohort soon after birth, and then again nine additional times from 1965 to 2014 with a number of different directors of research. A new survey of this group is planned for 2018 under the Direction of Alissa Goodman. The results were significant. They confirmed that the health of this population was closely related to resources associated with socio/relational factors—many of those listed in the table. But it also showed that those who overcame social disadvantages, did so as a result of a wide variety of relational resources. They included familial resources, such as parental determination to assure proper schooling, behavioral resources such as having a stable bed time, and personal resources such as gaining pleasure from recreational reading.

The Harvard Study of Adult Development began in 1938. It followed 700 men and some of their spouses for more than 75 years. Those subjects who are still alive are in their 90s. A second generation study has begun under the direction of Robert Waldinger and will follow children of the members of the first study. A major conclusion of the first study was that the greatest contributor to health into old age is strong loving relationships. People who maintained close family ties and good friendships for a very long time remained healthier and happier into old age than those who did not. The Harvard study is of the socio/relational resources of a particularly privileged group. They are the equivalent of Aristotle's full citizens who have the educational, financial, social and relational resources to live well and virtuous lives. Even at the top of the socio-economic scale there are dramatic differences in health that are dependent on the quality of relational interactions.

While Aristotle's understanding of a good life and Bentham's ideas about happiness help us see that health is only one of many contributors to personal happiness—to a good life—we also can now recognize that such resources contribute to our health. The social/relational model of health asserts that healthy human beings are not isolated minds in chemical/mechanical bodies but are people in the world who engage with others in many ways, in a wide array of settings, and with multiple purposes, which chief among them is the goal of a good and happy life. This view is increasingly reinforced by scientific research that describes the need for connections with others for healthy human development. Everything from brain development to emotional maturity depends on connections to other people. Unlike most other creatures, we cannot survive without a long period of supported early development; we cannot take care of ourselves as infants and we cannot develop as healthy adults without such connections.

As in all deep changes it will take a long time for this new model to be well understood, and, even when understood, there will be resistance to it because of the long success of the current chemical/mechanical model. There are some strong signs of acceptance. A large proportion of nurses and many primary care doctors have explicitly adopted a social/relational model of health well-being, considering social and relational factors in their assessment and treatment of patients. Hospitals have implicitly recognized the importance of connections to others by building new hospitals with single rooms to allow visiting at all hours and even overnight stay by relatives, whose presence contributes to recovery. The New England Journal of Medicine has formed an organization called NEJM Catalyst to create "practical innovations in health delivery." In turn, NEJM Catalyst sponsored a seminar called "Expanding the Bounds of Care Delivery: Integrating Mental Social and Physical Health." But there is still a very long way to go in policy development, in medical education, and especially in the public consciousness.

Medical education must begin developing a curriculum that extends beyond the chemical/mechanical model. Policy makers must come to see that resources for social wellbeing are fundamental responsibilities of the state, not merely contributors to health. Patients must come to recognize that medical care, fitness, and proper diet are only the chemical mechanical resources among many social/relational resources that are needed for a full and rewarding life. However, as members of the public, we must begin to see that health is only one of many contributors to a good and happy life—and certainly not the most critical one. This will be the most difficult transition because we have been mechanical patients for so long and have internalized the attitudes associated with it.

Because we are complex social beings, the very limited chemical/mechanical account of our bodies is deficient for understanding not only health, but also well-being. Both require a wide variety of resources that allow us to develop well-functioning connections to other people. We can conclude that our lives are better and healthier when we have adequate resources to develop and live well: making sure that such resources are available to all not only results in better and happier lives for everyone, but it also improves overall health.

Bibliography

The Annual Register, or a View of the History, Politics, and Literature, for the Year 1763. London: Printed for J. Dodsley, in Pall Mall. (1790). http://www.bodley.ox.ac.uk/cgi-bin/ilej/pbrowse.pl?item=vol&id=ar.1763.x.x.6.x&name=Volume+6&nv1=ILEJ.5.&nv2=Annual+Register (Accessed October 10, 2016).

Antonovsky, A. (1987). *Unraveling the Mystery of Health: How People Manage Stress and Stay Well*. New York: Jossey Bass.

Arikha, N. (2008). *Passions and Tempers: A History of the Humours*. New York: HarperCollins.

Aubrey, J. (1982). R. Barber (Ed.). *Brief Lives: A Modern English Version*. Woodbridge, Suffolk: The Boydell Press.

Bacon, F. (1909–1914). The New Atlantis. C. W. Eliot (Ed.). Vol. 3, Part 2, *The Harvard Classics*. New York: P.F. Collier & Son.

Bacon, F., Novum Organum; with Other Parts of the Great Instauration. (1994). J. Gibson and P. Peter Urbach (Eds.). Carus Student Editions; V. 3. Chicago: Open Court.

Bacon, F. (2003). *Historie Naturall and Experimentall, of Life and Death: Or of the Prolongation of Life*. Oxford: Text Creation Partnership, pp. 166–167.

Bentham, J. (1817). *Catechism of Parliamentary Reform; or, Outline of a Plan of Parliamentary Reform; in the Form of Question and Answer; With Reasons to Each Article*. Oxford: Oxford University.

Boyle, R. (1772). *The Works of the Honourable Robert Boyle in Six Volumes: To Which Is Prefixed the Life of the Author.* A New Edition. London: Printed for J. and F. Rivington L. Davis W. Johnston S. Crowder T. Payne [And 12 Others in London].

Burney F. Account from Paris of a terrible operation—1812 [letter to Esther Burney]. Henry W. and Albert A. Berg Collection. 22 March 1812. New York Public Library, New York. Online at the New Jacksonian Blog. http://newjacksonianblog.blogspot. ca/2010/12/breast cancer in 1811-Mme d'Arblay-burneys.html. (Accessed November 23, 2014).

Butterfield, H. (1965). *The Whig Interpretation of History.* New York: W.W. Norton & Company.

Bynum, W.F., and Porter, R. (Eds.). (1993). Companion Encyclopedia of the History of Medicine Vols. 1 and 2. London: Routledge Press.

The Canadian Index of Wellbeing, University of Waterloo. uwaterloo.ca/Canadian-index-wellbeing. (Accessed September 12, 2016).

Carpenter, K.J. (1986). *The History of Scurvy and Vitamin C.* Cambridge: Cambridge University Press.

Carson, R. (1992). *Silent Spring (With an Introduction by Al Gore).* New York: Houghton Mifflin.

Chadwick, E. (1842). *Sanitary Condition of the Labouring Population and on the Means of its Improvement.* London. W. Cloes and Sons.

Cohen, N. (1989). *Health and the Rise of Civilization.* London: Yale University Press, pp. 47–48.

Diamond, J. (2012). *The World Until Yesterday.* New York: Penguin Books.

Descartes, R. (1982). *Discourse on Method and Meditations* (1st ed.). Indianapolis: Bobbs-Merrill Educational Publishing, pp. 45, 61, 62, 574.

Doudna, J. (2015). Genome-editing revolution: My whirlwind year with CRISPR. *Nature.* 528: 469–471.

Duffin, J. (1999). *History of Medicine: A Scandalously Short Introduction.* Toronto: University of Toronto Press.

Elliott, J., Vaitilingam, R., and Elliott, J. (2008). *Now We Are Fifty: Key Findings from the National Child Development Study.* London. The Centre for Longitudinal Studies, Institute of Education, University of London.

Encyclopedia Britannica. (1911). Vol. 14. (11th ed.). London: Cambridge University Press, p. 517.

Flexner, A. (2015). *Medical Education in the United States and Canada: A Report to the Carnegie Foundation for the Advancement of Teaching.* New York: Sagwan Press.

Foucault, M. (1973). *The Birth of the Clinic: An Archaeology of Medical Perception* (A. M. S. Smith, Trans.). New York: Vintage Books, p. 27.

Gawande, A. (2014). *Being Mortal.* Toronto, Doubleday Canada.

Glouberman, S. (Ed.). (1996). *Beyond Restructuring: A Collection of Papers from the King's Fund International Seminar.* London: King's Fund.

Glouberman, S. (2001). *Towards a New Perspective on Health Policy.* Ottawa: Renouf Publishing.

Glouberman, S. and Millar, J. (1993). Evolution of the determinants of health, health policy, and health information systems in Canada. *American Journal of Public Health* 93(3): 388–392.

Gould, S.J. (2002). *The Structure of Evolutionary Theory.* Cambridge: The Belknap Press of Harvard University Press.

Gubrium, J. (1975). *Living and Dying in Murray Manor.* New York. St. Martin's Press.

Guthrie, D. (1945). *A History of Medicine.* Toronto: Thomas Nelson and Sons.

Hart, S. (2008). *Brain, Attachment, Personality: An Introduction to Neuroaffective Development.* London. Karnac Books.

Hobbes, T. (2008). Leviathan. J.C.A. Gaskin (Ed.). Oxford: Oxford University Press.

Hoffenberg, R. (2001). Christiaan Barnard: His first transplants and their impact on concepts of death. *BMJ.* 323(7327): 1478–1480.

Hornsby, J.A. and Schmidt, R.E. (1914). *The Modern Hospital: Its Inspiration, Its Architecture, Its Equipment, Its Operation.* Philadelphia, PA: W.B. Saunders.

Horwich, P. (2012). *Wittgenstein's Metaphilosophy.* Oxford: Oxford University Press.

Howard, J. and Strauss, A. (Eds.). (1975). *Humanizing Health Care.* New York. Wiley.

Hunter, M. (1990). Alchemy, magic and moralism in the thought of Robert Boyle. *British Journal for the History of Science* 23: 387–410.

Hunter, M. (Ed.). (1994). *Robert Boyle by Himself and His Friends.* London: William Pickering.

Hunter, M. (2000). *Robert Boyle (1627–1691): Scrupulosity and Science*. Woodbridge: The Boydell Press.

Hunter, M. (2009). *Boyle between God and Science*. New Haven, CT: Yale University Press.

Hunter, M., Clericuzio, A., and Principe, L.M. (Eds.). (2001). *The Correspondence of Robert Boyle*. Vol. 2: 1662–1665. London: Pickering & Chatto.

Hunter, M., Clericuzio, A., and Principe, L.M. (Eds.). (2001). *The Correspondence of Robert Boyle*. Vol. 6: 1684–1691, Appendices, Index. London: Pickering & Chatto.

Hunter, M., and Davis, E. B. (Eds.). (1999). *The Works of Robert Boyle*. Vols. 1, 2 and 3: General Introduction, Textual Note, Publications to 1660. London: Pickering & Chatto.

Hunter, M., and Schaffer, S. (1989). *Robert Hooke: New Studies*. Woodbridge, England: The Boydell Press.

Illich, I. (1975). *Medical Nemesis: The Expropriation of Health*. New York: Pantheon Books.

Jardine, L. (2003). *The Curious Life of Robert Hooke: The Man Who Measured London*. London: HarperCollins.

Jenkins, A. (2013). *Learning and the Lifecourse*. London. The Centre for Longitudinal Studies Institute of Education, University of London.

Jenner, E. (1798). *An Inquiry into the Causes and Effects of the Variolæ Vaccinæ, or Cow-Pox*. www.bartleby.com/38/4/1.html. (Accessed December 6, 2017).

Kennedy, E.M. (1972). *In Critical Condition: The Crisis in America's Health Care*. New York: Simon and Shuster.

Keys, A. (1955). Obesity and heart disease. *Journal of Clinical Epidemiology* 1: 456–461.

Klawans, H.L. (1982). *The Medicine of History from Paracelsus to Freud*. New York: Raven Press.

Kuhn, T.S. (1962). *The Structure of Scientific Revolutions*. Chicago: University of Chicago Press.

Lalonde, M. (1974). *A New Perspective on the Health of Canadians*. Ottawa: Government of Canada.

LeFanu, J. (1999). *The Rise and Fall of Modern Medicine*. London: Little, Brown and Company.

Locke, J. (1975). *An Essay Concerning Human Understanding*. Peter H. Nidditch (Ed.). Oxford: Oxford University Press.

Locke, J. (1976–1989). *The Correspondence of John Locke*, 8 vols. E. S. de Beer (Ed.). Oxford: Oxford University Press.

Locke, J. (2006). *An Essay Concerning Toleration and Other Writings on Law and Politics, 1667–1683.* J. R. Milton and P. Milton (Eds.). Oxford: Oxford University Press.

McKnight, J. (1986). Demedicalization and possiblilities for health. In *The Living Economy: A New Economic in the Making.* P. Ekins (Ed.). London and New York: Routledge and Kegan Paul.

Milton, J.R. (2001). Locke, medicine and the mechanical philosophy. *British Journal for the History of Philosophy* 9, no. 2: 221–243.

Mukherjee, S. (2010). *The Emperor of All Maladies.* New York: Scribner A Division of Simon & Schuster.

Mukherjee, S. (2016). *The Gene: An Intimate History.* New York: Scribner.

Newman, W. R., and Grafton, A. (2001). Introduction: The problematic status of astrology and alchemy in premodern Europe. In *Secrets of Nature: Astrology and Alchemy in Early Modern Europe.* W. R. Newman and A. Grafton (Eds.). Cambridge: The MIT Press.

Newman, W.R., and Principe, L.M. (2002). *Alchemy Tried in the Fire: Starkey, Boyle and the Fate of Helmontian Chymistry.* Chicago: University of Chicago Press.

Newton, I. (1975). The Correspondence of Isaac Newton. A. Rupert Hall and L. Tilling (Eds.). Vols. I to VII. 1709–1713. Cambridge: Published for the Royal Society at the University Press.

Piketty, T. (2014). *Capital in the Twenty-First Century.* Cambridge, MA: Belknap Press.

Pinker, S. (2002). *The Blank Slate: The Modern Denial of Human Nature.* London: Penguin Books.

Porter, R. (2002). *Blood and Guts: A Short History of Medicine.* London: Penguin Books.

Porter, R. (1997). *The Greatest Benefit to Mankind: A Medical History of Humanity from Antiquity to the Present.* London: HarperCollins.

Porter, R, and Porter, D. (1966). *In Sickness and in Health.* London: Fourth Estate.

Reznek, L. (1966). *The Nature of Disease.* London: Routledge & Kegan Paul.

Riley, J.C. (1987). Disease without death: New sources for a history of sickness. *Journal of Interdisciplinary History* 17, no. 3: 537–563.

Semmelweis, I. (1983). *Etiology, Concept and Prophylaxis of Childbed Fever (History of Science and Medicine)*. Translated by K. Codell Carter. Madison, WI: University of Wisconsin Press.

Sen, A. (1985). *Commodities and Capabilities* (1st ed.). New York: Elsevier.

Shapin, S. (1996). *The Scientific Revolution*. Chicago: The University of Chicago Press.

Shapin, S., and Schaffer, S. (1985). *Leviathan and the Air-Pump: Hobbes, Boyle, and the Experimental Life (Including a Translation of Thomas Hobbes, Dialogus Physicus De Natura Aeris, by Simon Schaffer)*. Princeton: Princeton University Press.

Singer, C., and Ashworth Underwood, E. (1962). *A Short History of Medicine*. Oxford: Clarendon Press.

Skloot, R. (2010). *The Immortal Life of Henrietta Lacks*. New York: Random House.

Smith, R. (2002). In search of "non-disease." *British Medical Journal* 324, no. 7342: 883–885.

Spencer, H. (1904). *An Autobiography*. London. Willams and Norgate.

Stern, B. J. (1941). *Society and Medical Progress*. Princeton: Princeton University Press.

Welch, H.G., Schwartz, L.M., and Woloshin, S. (2015) *Overdiagnosed: Making People Sick in the Pursuit of Health*. Boston, MA: Beacon Press.

Williams, S.J. (2003). *Medicine and the Body*. London: SAGE Publications.

Winslow, C.E.A. (1952). *Man and Epidemics*. Princeton: Princeton University Press.

Wittgenstein, L. (1951). *Philosophical Investigations*. Oxford. Basil Blackwell.

Wootton, D. (2006). *Bad Medicine*. Oxford University Press.

World Health Organization. (2014). *Noncommunicable Diseases Country Profiles*. Switzerland: World Health Organization.

Index